24 Days

24 Days

Following the Nile on Foot

Jomana Ismail

BInk *Bink Books*

Bedazzled Ink Publishing Company • Fairfield, California

paperback 978-1-949290-30-1

Cover photo
by
Hend Gamil

Cover Design
by
Hend Gamil

Sappling

Studio

Bink Books
a division of
Bedazzled Ink Publishing, LLC
Fairfield, California
http://www.bedazzledink.com

For mum and dad,
They always supported me
even when they didn't understand what I was doing

Author's Note

To write this book I relied on my memory of the events it alludes to, researched facts and consulted the person that the lead character of the book is based on. I have changed the names of all the individuals mentioned, and in some cases I modified details that could identify them, in addition to creating two characters to preserve anonymity. The order of a few events has been changed to avoid narrating unnecessary details and to accentuate the experience, and I omitted people and events when they had no impact on the storyline. This book is my perspective of events and therefore, by definition, subjective.

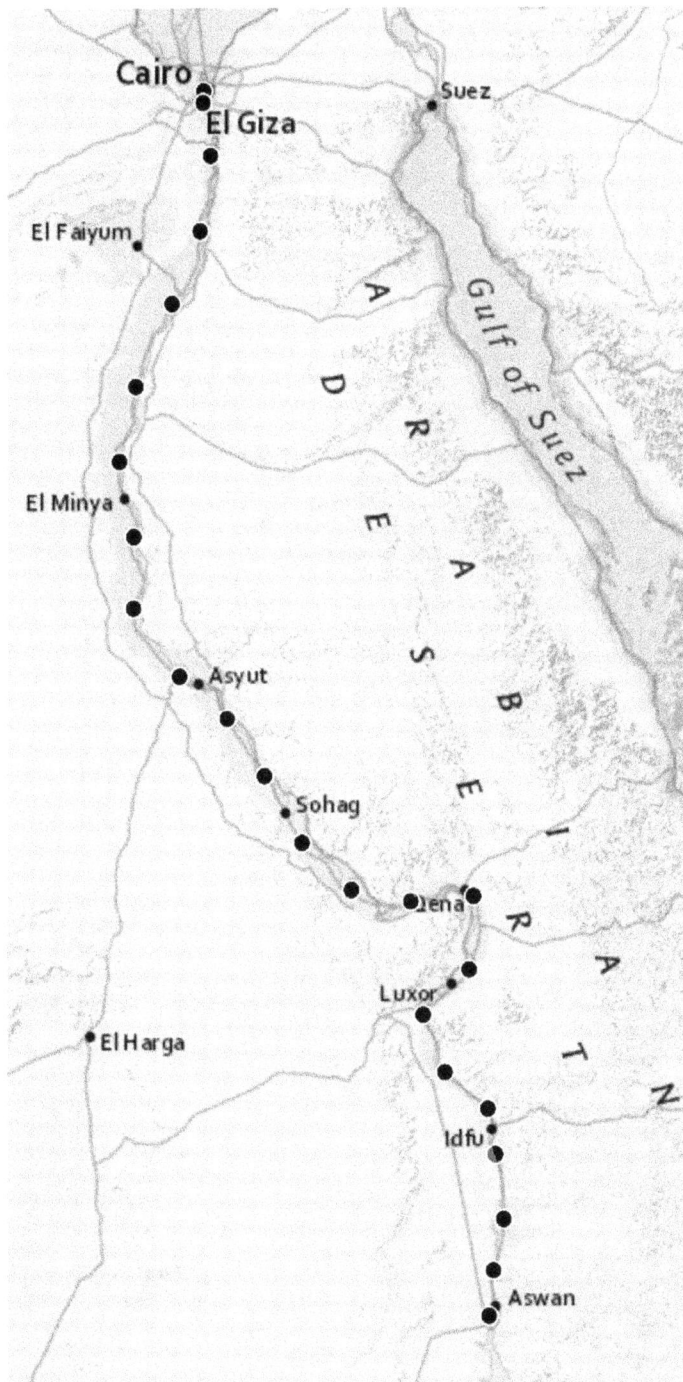

Cairo

El Giza

Suez

El Faiyum

Gulf of Suez

El Minya

Asyut

Sohag

Qena

Luxor

El Harga

Idfu

Aswan

EASTERN

DESERT

Part 1

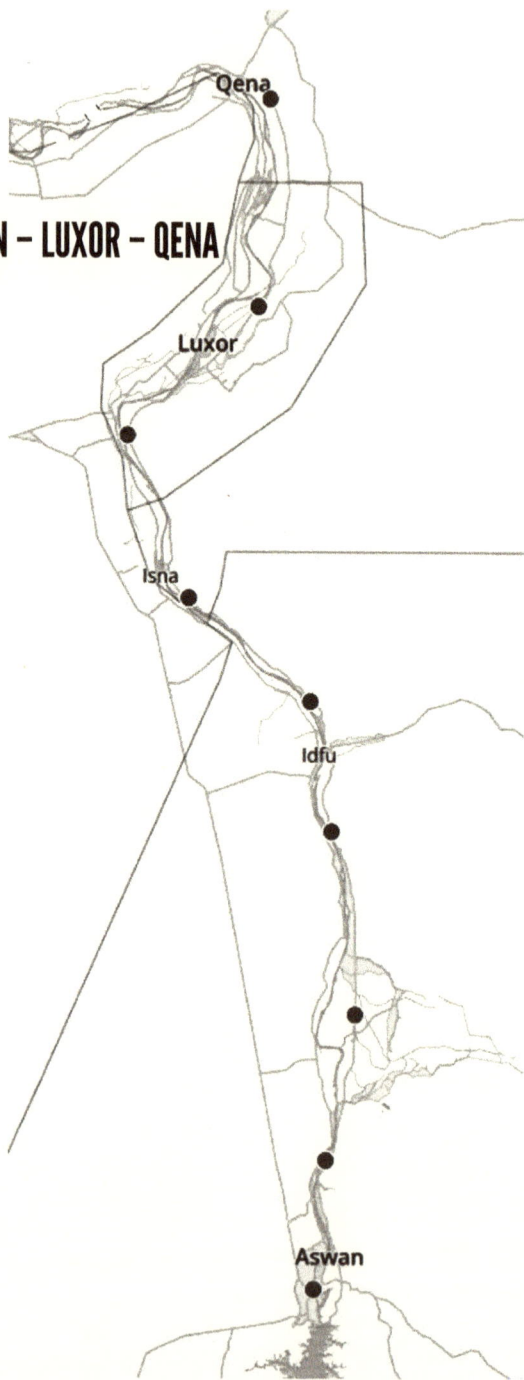

Part 1
ASWAN – LUXOR – QENA

25,000 FEET ABOVE sea level at two am, with my eyes closed, thinking about what I had left behind and what was ahead of me. I had just resigned, was feeling lost and my heart was drumbeating for the coming adventure. The thought of walking with three guys I barely knew for twenty-four days was confusing me, the idea of doing this in very conservative cities was alarming me and the question of why I was choosing to do this was running through my head relentlessly, but my excitement at walking with new friends in cities I had never visited before, challenging myself, was also overwhelming in the best possible way.

The many tangled thoughts in my head kept me from sleeping and in an effort to at least calm them down I started writing thank you messages to the people who had been great sources of support to me, even if they hadn't known it at the time. I wrote to a friend who was always encouraging me when everyone else was cynical and I wrote to three men I had a less obvious connection with.

One of them inspired me to do whatever makes me feel that I am being true to myself. Another had a positive indirect effect on me; he had a farm and I had wanted to learn basic agricultural skills, so I had a weekly ritual of going to his farm to help and learn. The farm became an outlet for me, a way of disconnecting from a reality that I didn't always know how to deal with, but my time there also made me able to think more clearly for the rest of the week. The third man had a smile that made me feel that life would always be good, no matter what. I needed to thank them and on a subconscious level I think I also wanted to be comforted. The effect that people may have on us can be heartwarming.

I had previously worked as a Startup Space Manager and I used to joke about whether "space" referred to an empty place or the expanse full of stars that lies beyond the earth. In the end, I thought it had more of the first meaning and that was why I resigned. When I sent messages to various people telling them what I had done, most of the responses were "congratulations." Apparently many people feel that if someone resigns from their job, he or she has been able to break the cage and fly. And without a doubt that was true for me. For several months beforehand, I had been suffocating and becoming more depressed, day after day. After my resignation, I met one of the people who had congratulated me and I found out that he was planning to undertake an awesome challenge. I had always wanted to travel more locally, discovering my own country more fully, and it seemed this possibility could be just a few steps away for me.

I live in Cairo, Egypt's capital. True, it has all kinds of people but as often happens in big capital cities when people immigrate there, it is the people who adapt to the norms of the place, often showing the worst versions of themselves to be able to survive in the most competitive city in the country. When I travel for vacations I usually go to coastal cities, but these don't fully represent Egypt or Egyptians either. They are mainly vacation destinations and in them we see perhaps the best versions of people because we go there to relax. I always felt that I didn't know much about Egypt or the Egyptians; I could only talk about Cairo and Cairenes. But that was about to change. Unattached, I had the freedom to be spontaneous.

My friend was preparing for a challenge: to cross Egypt on foot to raise awareness about issues related to population growth. In essence, three men were going to walk from Aswan to Cairo along the Nile. This would entail passing through nine governorates, each governorate containing a big city, a few small cities, and many villages. I had been to some of the big cities before but definitely not on foot. Walking the nine governorates would mean covering 934 km, the estimated distance. Moreover, they had set a timeframe of twenty-four days to complete the entire walk, which broken down would mean covering an average of 43 km per day, around nine hours of walking. Upon discovering that, my interest and excitement were piqued but the trip was due to start in fifteen days and I wasn't physically prepared. So I told my friend that I wanted to join the trip, that I wouldn't be able to complete the entire distance but that I could walk for something like 10 km per day. My friend, Ahmed, told me that he would ask the sponsors if this would be acceptable.

After a few days, Ahmed told me that I needed to meet the main sponsor who then, when I met him, approved me joining even if it was just to meet the youth at their centers to participate in the activities planned as part of their awareness raising campaign. After the meeting I called Ahmed, excited, and told him that I was in and he replied in an overbearing tone that someone must have done me a great favor; he was of course talking about himself.

After writing the messages, I could see the sun was starting to rise. I was sitting on a window seat on the left just after the wing on an airplane heading to Aswan. The sunlight revealed the scenery that I had been so eager to see. This scenery would be our surroundings for the next twenty-four days. Osama was sitting beside me; we looked at each other and laughed.

"Is that what we are going to walk through?" I asked and we couldn't control our laughter for several minutes.

We saw an expanse of wide desert and narrow curving river. The river in fact would be our compass, as the plan was to walk along the Nile from Egypt's most southern city and head north; we were going to walk with the current of the river. The view from above suggested that the landscape was purely arid desert but the closer we got to the ground the richer we found it to be.

Osama was one of the three men planning to walk the 934 km. He was twenty-one years old and still studying at college, a well-built man and tall, with light brown hair, a full beard, and honey-colored hooded eyes framed by long eyelashes and thick arched eyebrows. His long curly hair was always styled upwards so it looked a bit like a lion's mane. This I associated with his personality, which is strong and courageous but also impulsive.

I met Osama only eight days before our trip and we didn't start off very well. We were at a meeting with the main sponsors of our adventure. He was dressed in very loose grey sweat pants and a shirt. He was silent when we were at the meetings but extremely restless, moving all around, when the meetings were over. He also talked too much about anything and everything and he made fun of everything, himself included.

When the meetings were over, I drove him back home and we had a more serious conversation. He told me about his studies, a bit about his childhood and his life aspirations. Osama was studying Computer Science at a private university and things weren't going well. He had entered into a fight defending one of his classmates whom he saw as being treated unfairly, although he didn't know what the problem was. He just got into the fight without even knowing who he was fighting with; it turned out that his opponent was the owner of the college and this got Osama suspended for the year. Earlier in his life, when he was a teenager, he had chosen to move out of his parents' house and had to earn his living; he worked mainly in the tourism industry which had given him the chance to travel a lot and find an outlet for his enormous energy and great aspirations. His dream was to be an astrophysicist.

We arrived at his drop off point and I found myself thinking that he was a nice person after all and feeling good that I already knew two of the three guys I would be staying with for this period of adventure. We had another meeting arranged for the next day at eleven am in Maadi, a residential area in south east Cairo, and we agreed to meet before that in Heliopolis, another distinct area in east Cairo at six am, to go walking.

The guys had already been training for the challenge for six months by walking across cities and even traveling on foot. I, too, wanted to use the ten days before we were due to travel to Aswan to train for the challenge. Since I was a child I have always played sports. I took part in artistic gymnastics until I was twelve, then tried volleyball, basketball, tennis, swimming, athletics, and shooting and was on the club teams for most. I had focused on cycling for a while, until an incident one day where a police dog came running after me as I was cycling along a public road. I glanced behind to see what was happening, lost my course, and rode up a pile of sand, flying away from the bike like Chuck from Angry Birds, going faster as I approached the ground and landing on my right shoulder, finally lying bruised on the sand. And that was my last experience with cycling. Later I started regularly hiking, swimming, and running. So even though I hadn't been training for the challenge, I had physical fitness.

Egypt has its own attitudes to time, with frequent traffic jams making it difficult to always be punctual but lateness also often being an accepted part of the culture. But there are many people who react quite strongly to this.

The next day, I texted Osama saying that I would be half an hour late. I arrived at six-thirty am and he came ten minutes later. We started walking briskly, so that we would still be able to catch the meeting. He wasn't in the best of moods but neither was I, as I hadn't had my morning coffee which is important for me to start functioning. We walked at an average pace of 6 km/hr. He started to express his frustration in the middle, telling me this was because I had been late in arriving. Though I didn't reply, I wanted to tell him that he had arrived later than me. He continued, "I don't like being late."

We kept walking quickly and quietly, until we no longer knew which way to go but tried a couple of ways until we found the right one. All this time we had been walking along Salah Salem, which after a while became El Nasr road—two fast roads with high rates of traffic and pollution. We came across a construction area in El Nasr road and suddenly I found myself skating over wet gypsum, swinging to the right and left until I regained my balance and stepped out of the slippery area with my shoes covered in gypsum. All was over in a few seconds and Osama couldn't save me; it had seemed certain that I was going to fall but in the end I hadn't so we laughed and things started to feel more normal between us again.

We passed by a street that I had gone down many times before but always in a car. Going this time on foot, I discovered that it was full of treasures. It is like a flea market, containing things I couldn't imagine existing—antique doors and windows that could be easily fixed and many other used things. Surveying it from a bridge, we stopped for a moment to savour its atmosphere, having walked 14 km that day and with 5 km left.

I was getting tired, thirsty, and drained. When we found a kiosk, I bought water and a snack, then sat on the street side for five minutes reenergizing. Upon reaching a crossroad, I used Google maps to check the best route. Osama didn't like the shortest one because it involved walking through slums, so we took the second fastest route. We crossed the street under El Moneeb bridge and had to climb over a fence. This wasn't easy for me because I was wearing a backpack so Osama offered to carry it and, wanting to be gentlemanly, he refused to give it back until we arrived. The route we took ended up taking us through a downmarket area, El Basateen. We found ourselves walking along a narrow busy road with red brick houses on either side, people wearing jilbab (long, loose garments), and herds of animals in the street. Osama wasn't happy about this while I, on the other hand, appreciated the novelty of the goats welcoming us on the way and the horses eating in the middle of the street.

"Of course, it seems that you are not used to seeing this but I sleep in their laps," he said.

I thought he was exaggerating and had no idea to what extent he could be speaking the truth.

We reached the meeting place and I changed into clean clothes. We were meeting other sponsors for the adventure. Ahmed was always in these meetings—he was leading and he acted like a godfather who wanted to get the most benefits for us. At twenty-six, he was of average height with fair skin, brown downturned eyes, thin pink lips, and a snub nose. I never saw his round face with a beard or mustache, his skin was always smooth.

When I first decided to join the guys, I went for a practice walk with Ahmed to start preparing myself for the challenge. I had known him for nine years and there is a five-year age difference between us so I had witnessed him growing up and becoming a leading figure in the sports field. We talked about the plan and our respective expectations and Ahmed was keen to tell me about the other two guys, Osama and Younes. He had known Osama for a long time, they used to play parkour together and do some scouting activities. But he hadn't known Younes for long. Younes had been working in a company that wanted to organize a sports event for its employees and Ahmed worked with them as a freelancer to help with the event's organization. When the idea of the challenge was raised, they reconnected to undertake it together.

Ahmed told me that Younes was a bit different. Younes has strong feelings for Egypt and maybe that's because he is from a big family that is well connected to the government. Ahmed thought that the problem is that Younes didn't feel the suffering of the people of the middle and lower classes of Egypt. I love Egypt as well and I didn't really understand what the problem was; for me, loving a country is about a feeling of belonging and not about social classes.

In Egypt, there is a clear separation of social classes, with each having its own places to live, spend our time, or go on vacation, as if we lived parallel lives. This often alienates us from one another, with the lower classes usually regarding the upper class as unimaginably privileged and any obstacle as being removed because of their status. Meanwhile, the upper classes usually view the lower classes as hindering the progress of the country through ignorance, and keeping birth rates high. Despite that, we were all connected once for the love of the country. In Tahrir Square, during the 2011 revolution, all social classes were represented, and all were calling for bread, freedom, and social justice. We all cared for each other and we all wanted the best for our country during this time, recognizing what I believe is a profound truth: there is no contradiction between being part of whichever social class each belongs to and all of us loving our country.

I heard another perspective again about Younes from Osama. When the three of us were shopping for the trip, Osama started imitating his distinctive straight-backed walk, where he looks up, placing his heels on the ground first then rising up onto his tiptoes. Then Osama talked about meetings between the three of them where Younes would suddenly ask "is that all?" before preparing to leave. Osama and Ahmed thought this was part of his arrogance but, having attended meetings with them, I knew how they could extend for no obvious reason. I told the guys that I would be more like Younes after the challenge. But to be honest, I was a bit worried. I wanted to be on good terms with everyone and it seemed that Younes would not be easy. I asked my friends what their thoughts were on how to deal with him. I told them that he seemed a little aloof—maybe cocky—and I wasn't sure whether to imitate his attitude or to be friendly. I thought that sometimes people with attitude would relate more to others with attitude. My friends, more than anything, were excited that I do this experiment and eager to see the results.

The four of us were on a Whatsapp group so we could communicate and coordinate. Younes was going on two trips before our big trip together—one shorter hiking tour and then a workshop in the US. So I was going to meet him for the first time on the first day of the adventure. Because he was away, he repeatedly asked for updates and at first Ahmed responded, but always late at night or on the day following Younes' question. As I started to get more involved with the trip preparations, I suggested that if Ahmed was busy perhaps I could respond to him instead. From these first small interactions, where I would respond and he would thank me, I realized that I felt comfortable dealing with him. Do you think this is crazy?

The day before he arrived, I wrote to him in the group that I was excited to see him the next day and he replied that he felt the same. And then I totally forgot about the plan. Of course, the four of us traveling together would prove to be the unexpected step that would unfold our outer layers and reveal our true natures.

Day 1

I WOKE UP at four am and opened the curtains but it was still dark outside. We were staying in a hotel by the Nile, Helnan Aswan, and the previous day my room had been bright with a spectacular view. I was on the first floor and, from the window, I saw the blue of the Nile with white sailing boats floating with the current. There was a pool and gardens in the foreground and small yellow mountains in the background. It was a nice start to the adventure.

We were due to meet at the restaurant at five to start our walk at six. Our daily routine had already been meticulously planned. We wanted to start with the sunrise to finish our daily walk sometime before sunset and have some time to see each town or city we passed through. The event management company had booked all our hotels for the twenty-four days and we had prepared and shared a nutrition plan with them. We had two cars that would accompany us, one for the four of us in case we needed it and for our physiotherapist, and one for the support team: a videographer, a social media expert, a coordinator who would oversee interactions between us and the young people joining our walks and finally the event management company team: Managing Director Hamdy and his associates, Ramzy and Samy.

At the restaurant I was the first to arrive and Nadia El Adany followed closely, then Younes, then Ahmed and Osama. The event management team was already there. We ate a carb-rich breakfast of mashed potatoes and mashed sweet potatoes, I had a coffee with milk and there were breakfast boxes ready for us to take.

Nadia is a renowned athlete and very active on social media. She was joining us for the first day and the last eight days of the walk to publicize the challenge. Having met Nadia once in one of the preparation meetings, I was so happy she was joining; I really felt the need for another woman's support. By contrast, Ahmed told me before I met her that she had an attitude and that he would have preferred someone else to join. And this was the first time I got the impression that he wasn't in control of everything, in spite of the impression he was trying to convey.

Nadia was a short, slim woman with strong core and leg muscles and curly brown hair framed her round face and green eyes. At the first meeting, we were at the office of one of our sponsors, undergoing a fitness test and being equipped with heart rate straps to monitor our cardiac activity during the walk. She immediately sat, without greeting our sponsor or any of us. After a moment of awkward silence, everyone introduced themselves and then we had to leave for our Body Mass Index (BMI) and stress tests and she for other meetings. Before leaving she had started to mingle a little, celebrating the fact that a woman would be joining the three men in this adventure. I liked her; I thought she was genuine and very supportive.

So on that first morning, we all sat eating breakfast and talking about very general things. I was quiet, unused as I was to waking up this early, and finding everything and almost everyone new and was somewhat overwhelming. I was also a bit worried. I had a problem with my right knee that had bothered me almost all my life. Aged fourteen, I noticed that when I took part in athletics events it always felt unstable and when I ran for long distances it hurt. Several doctors told me that I had osteoarthritis and gave me medications that never helped. When I turned twenty-seven, I traveled to Leipzig to do my Masters and in my second week there I went hiking with some classmates. When I went home, my knee hurt like never before. I wanted to see a doctor and the first appointment that could be booked for me was a seemingly endless two weeks away. I couldn't ride my bike and climbed the stairs with difficulty. When I finally saw the doctor he did some scans and some physical tests. My issues with understanding German and his with speaking English impeded our communication, but what I understood was that I had a severe problem that might require an operation. No medication could cure it but we were going to do physiotherapy.

After six physiotherapy sessions, I already felt better—almost back to how I was before the hike. My main transportation in Leipzig was by bike. Cycling uphill hurt but I lived with it until the week before I left Germany for good. I went to a Syrian doctor in Berlin who told me that my problem was minor. My leg has an inward inclination which makes me put extra weight on the left part of the knee, causing the pain. The solution, he told me, was to wear an in-sole and he took my foot measurements in order to send me one, though he never did.

Before the trip, I went to the physiotherapist that would be accompanying us. I wanted him to have a look at my knee because it had started to hurt after all the walking that I did in preparation. He did some massage therapy but by the time I left it was hurting more than when I had arrived. Secretly, I was afraid that this journey would harm my knee more and perhaps cause a serious injury.

Assembled, we took our breakfast boxes and got into the cars to ride to our starting point. We had two cars, both Toyota Land Cruiser Prado make. The car would turn out to be an important aspect of our journey. It is supposed to have five seats, but the fifth is a third row seat by the back door and not comfortable for long distances. On this day, Nadia and I sat on the front seat together, the guys on the back seat and Mohsen, the physiotherapist, on the third row seat. We hit the road— it was fresh and a bit chilly by Egyptian standards, so I opened the window and sat on it, to enjoy the weather and let Nadia sit properly.

Approaching the high dam of Aswan, we all had wide smiles on our faces. It seemed like the blue was invading the universe, the color fading gradually to the very light orange of the early morning sky and touching the turquoise blue of the Nile. We stood on the wall of the bridge, watching the sun rise, then Younes took out the Egyptian flag from his bag and we all stood holding it, feeling proud of where we belong. At this moment it felt that we were all one, standing behind the flag and holding it together.

We all had the same outfit: sports pants, undershirt, shirt, and jacket. The sportswear came from one of our sponsors, the Egyptian apparel company Sprint Active Wear. All were designed for men and because I joined them at the last minute there was no design specifically for women. The shirt and jacket had the logos of our sponsors but not the Egyptian flag, which we had noticed because Younes had asked before arriving if our outfits would carry the flag.

Younes and I wear the same size: small. When we were trying on our jackets, he tried the small and I tried the medium and found it was too large for me. So he gave me the small and then found out that there was another jacket in small, which of course he took. His generous impulse moved me and I felt bad that I hadn't done the same but the truth is I didn't want to look like a penguin. The jacket was already long and thick and I am much shorter than the guys. I wasn't comfortable in the shirt either because it was too loose around the arms. I told Younes that I would send my shirts to get them taken in and asked if he would like the same to be done for him, but he looked at me and replied with confidence, "No, it's okay." Looking at his arms, he continued, "I have muscles." I laughed hard then realized he wasn't joking.

We took some photos on the bridge and I asked Younes for a selfie. I told him he was a celebrity; I was traveling with a Guinness Record holder. The two of us took a selfie, then the four of us. Then we all started walking.

Every one of us had a tracking mechanism, with all of us using mobile devices and Younes also using a Garmin watch. His watch was the most accurate so we used it as measurement of the distance covered.

There were always people from the support team walking with us. And in each governorate, students from the Faculty of Physical Education would join us for a day or two. On the first day, athletes from the Federation of Athletics of Aswan joined us. Before we traveled I had asked the organizers to ensure that girls would be able to walk with us during our journey. As I was joining, I thought that other women might be encouraged to join as well. They were very responsive and in Aswan there were dozens of men and four women accompanying us. I wasn't disappointed because the truth is, I wasn't sure beforehand that the young women would actually show up. To my delight, the students joined our walk and they were super excited for it. Doing sports in public is not something common in Upper Egypt.

I was walking in the back with the girls, as the path wound downhill with tall trees on each side. I wanted us to walk at the front but three of them were a little shy and reticent, so we stayed at the back and talked about their lives in Aswan. They told me that they would be considered bold for joining our walk. At almost the same height, around 160 cm, they all had beautiful hazelnut eyes and caramel skin. They wore sports pants, shirts, and head scarves though one was showing her hair.

One of the girls told me that she loved playing sports but that in her village she couldn't even walk on her own. Playing sports in public can be considered a disgrace in this part of the country. She was from Edfu and was staying in Aswan because of her studies. Her parents didn't mind that she lived on her own, nor did they forbid her from doing anything but the community judged her. She told me that she wanted to be a police officer when she graduated and to be accepted for this she would need to be fit. To be fit she would need to play sports. And to play sports she would need to be bold, would she be?

The students walked with us for five kilometers then they left and we continued. The Nile was sparkling on our left and the main road and city were on our right. There are no residential buildings on the main road, only public facilities; including a mall, school, mosque, café, hotels, and celebration halls. We kept walking until we found a sign that told us we were about to leave Aswan city and enter New Aswan city. Both are in the governorate of Aswan but they are very different. The former is an urban city while the latter is a rural one. This moment was weird in a good way, with the realization that I had crossed an entire city on foot and was starting a new one!

We were all together in the beginning, then Younes and Nadia started engaging in conversation and walking a bit slower than the rest of us. They seemed very enthusiastic about the topic they were discussing and Younes' facial and body movements were especially expressive. Something didn't feel right. The vibe between Younes and the other guys was cold, especially between him and Ahmed. Meanwhile, he was getting along very well with Nadia who he had just met. I was on the alert but not exactly worried, feeling that if anything went in a way that I didn't like I didn't have to be there.

Ahmed had set the pace at 5 kilometers per hour and Osama and I were following this pace. When we had walked a long way ahead of Younes and Nadia they started running until they reached us then they continued running to overtake us. Then they would wait for us and the cycle would begin again.

Ahmed came close to me and told me, "I don't like it when people change their words. He said that he wouldn't run but because of Nadia he changed his mind."

I was too tired to argue with him. My heart rate was over 150 beats per minute (bpm) and I could feel the rush of blood to my face, turning it red.

The path was straight most of the way, but as we entered New Aswan city there was a detour, a bridge over our heads and we weren't sure which road to take. The sun was above us too and we were getting hungry. I was wondering who knew the way. Pausing for a while under a bridge, I saw a small garden on the other side and went to stretch there, while Younes took charge of finding our path with the help of the police securing our walk.

As we resumed, the Nile was behind us and never ending agricultural fields stretched to our right and left. Then we started walking alongside the agricultural road, parallel to the Nile. To the left all was green and to the right a yellow hill was spotted with small houses. But all was pale because the sunlight was stronger than any color.

Ahmed came over and told me that I shouldn't stretch in the middle of the walk. His reasoning was not clear but when I told him I had to stretch, due to muscle strain, he surmised that I must be walking faster than the pace I should. Then he called the event management team to ask when the food was coming and it turned out that we still had an hour at least to wait.

After we had covered 10 km, around two hours of walking, a local TV channel came to cover the challenge. While they were shooting, each one of the five of us talked about our individual motivation for joining this challenge and how it had all started. I found Nadia asserting that the challenge was Younes's idea. Although no one disagreed with her publicly, I was thinking that this wasn't the information that had initially reached me. When I had first met with Ahmed, after resigning from my job, and he told me about the challenge somehow I had understood it to be both his and Younes's idea. After Nadia stated so clearly that it was Younes's idea, the TV anchor turned all his attention to Younes, asking him how he had come up with it in the first place.

Younes is a Guinness Record holder as a member of the fastest team to cross Europe by bicycle[1], which they did to raise awareness on autism. When he returned to Egypt he wanted to do another sports challenge for a cause, he thought that cycling would be too short of a trip so he decided to cross the country walking. Younes had contacted Ahmed and they found a sponsor with a cause; raising awareness on

---

1 In June 2017, Helmy Elsaeed with a Swedish team set a new Guinness World Record as the fastest team to cycle across Europe together.

population problems in the cities we were passing by. I thought of how glad I was to have been set straight on how the challenge had started. I was quite sure in my mind that Younes was the idea person and Ahmed was leading the operations.

After the break, Osama approached me and told me that since we had completed 10 km I should stop, as this is what we had agreed upon on so I wouldn't get injured. Though I started to object, Ahmed came over and reiterated Osama's words. I felt unsure. I was tired, my knees hurt and my heart rate was extremely high—almost in the danger zone[2]. I thought for a couple of seconds. I had done my due for the day but I felt that I could still walk more so after a short pause I told them, "Since I'll rest sooner or later, I'd rather rest when I can't continue walking." I could see that Osama was on the brink of arguing but Ahmed told him to leave me to do what I preferred. Everyone else was aiming to walk the whole distance and I felt that I wanted to test my limits and also to continue the story. So this is what I did.

On this day we walked for 22 km, which took us five and a half hours. Each of us marked where we stopped on Google maps. I sat on the ground in front of our car, trying to find shade, then Nadia came to sit beside me after posting an Instagram story of me all tired, with my face red, happy and glowing from the exercise. The boys tried to find a place to sit in the shade of the car as well; we were all clustered together in a small space of two by one meters on the ground. But in another five minutes we were ready to go.

We took the cars and returned to our hotel. On our way back, Mohsen couldn't sit in the back seat again because it was uncomfortable so he rode with the support team. Osama sat in the third row seat, Nadia in the front seat, while Younes, Ahmed, and I were in the back seat. On the way, Nadia put on her music and it was very energetic—like music for working out—and Osama moved his head in time with the music. And Nadia and Younes talked about missed chances, or stolen ideas. Both of them had been in the endurance sports field for a while and they had dreams and ideas about new challenges. Each of them had had the experience of either being ignored because of the fear of competition or having had their ideas stolen. Nadia had suggested to one of the first

2 Each individual has a maximum heart rate while exercising that, if we approach it, will increase the risk of a cardiac event.

people to climb Mount Everest that they do a hike together, tackling one of the big seven, but apparently he totally ignored her. I found this sad, feeling that people in this field should have the spirit to support others. These challenges should be for personal discovery and growth, not for breaking records.

Younes had also had a negative interaction with another endurance athlete, whom he had approached with the idea of crossing the Atlantic Ocean together on a raft. The man had expressed a lot of enthusiasm and Younes had shared some contacts with him to make it happen, but then he had attempted the challenge alone, without even writing to Younes to apologize. I told them that I saw this kind of behavior as killing the spirit of these challenges.

Younes looked at me over Ahmed and quickly replied, "I totally agree."

We reached the hotel and each went to our room, then I went to Ahmed to pick up some supplies. As I was about to leave, he looked at me from above and told me, "you can do it," tapping me twice on my left shoulder. I thanked him hesitantly and went to my room. He then messaged our WhatsApp group to suggest that we meet at eight-thirty in the lobby for dinner and asked Mohsen to visit him in his room for a physiotherapy session before dinner. So it seemed that the guys were planning to have their sessions in their rooms and meanwhile I didn't know what to do for my knees. I couldn't ask Mohsen to come to my room—it wouldn't feel appropriate—but he had told me that he should tape[3] my knees, so I needed to find a place for that.

I went to the lobby ten minutes late. Younes came and we talked for a bit before I realized that he reminded me of someone. He was talking like a celebrity who has a TV show where he pretends to be an Italian, interviewing Egyptian celebrities. The celebrity spoke little Arabic in the show and maybe that's why Younes reminded me of him; his Arabic sounded almost as though it came from a non-native speaker. Osama arrived, then Nadia, and finally Ahmed and we were ready to go for dinner. Ahmed had a skateboard that I was playing with, but Osama

---

3 Kinesiology tape is a thin, stretchy, elastic cotton strip with an acrylic adhesive. Therapeutic kinesiology tape that can benefit a wide variety of musculoskeletal and sports injuries, plus inflammatory conditions. (https:// physioworks.com.au)

wanted it as well, so to convince me to give it to him he warned me that I may get injured. I knew he was tricking me but I still left it to him.

We went to a hotel overviewing the Nile, the Movenpick Resort Aswan. We took a boat to go there but we didn't sit outside by the Nile, we sat instead in the restaurant and thinking maybe we would see the Nile through the glass windows in the morning. We were very hungry but I was too tired to eat and everything seemed dark. I was still not feeling well because of my elevated heart rate, but I knew that I had to eat. I took a small portion of food on my plate but couldn't finish it. Everyone liked the food so much, but as always, when compared to my mum's food I didn't find it that tasty.

I was sitting in the middle left of the table, with Nadia just in front of me, Osama on my left, Younes at the head of the table on my left and Ahmed on the other side of the table with the support team. Hamdy from the event management team asked my age and they didn't believe that I was thirty-one. I look much younger. We found out that Nadia was thirty-eight. I already knew that Osama was twenty-one and Younes now told us that he was twenty-eight. He also talked a bit about his family. He has a younger sister and he is very close to his mum, who is youthful and really looks like she could be his elder sister. We didn't ask Hamdy's age, but he looked to be in his early forties, with fair skin and a round face. Hamdy told us that he had a chubby ten-year-old kid whose favorite food was McDonalds and because Hamdy can't say no to him they always have it at home.

I was getting sleepy and Nadia wanted to leave because she had a flight in the early morning. We stood up but others were still engaged in conversation and didn't seem worried about getting up early the next day. While we waited for the guys outside the restaurant, Nadia asked me if I was engaged and I replied in the negative. She told me that she had been engaged once and speculated that maybe it was when they left each other that she felt the flame that had made her so enthusiastic about sports and ready to take her talent to the next level. I asked her if it was difficult to find a partner, given her job as a trainer and a triathlete, and she replied that she believes that when something is meant to be it happens, no matter the circumstances.

We said goodbyes and she prepared to leave for the hotel, telling me that she couldn't wait for the rest of the team, but then we found them coming and we all left together. I went to bed, hoping that I would wake up in the morning feeling well. I didn't want to stop after this first day.

Day 1
ASWAN
Aswan, New Aswan
22km – 4h 12m walking time

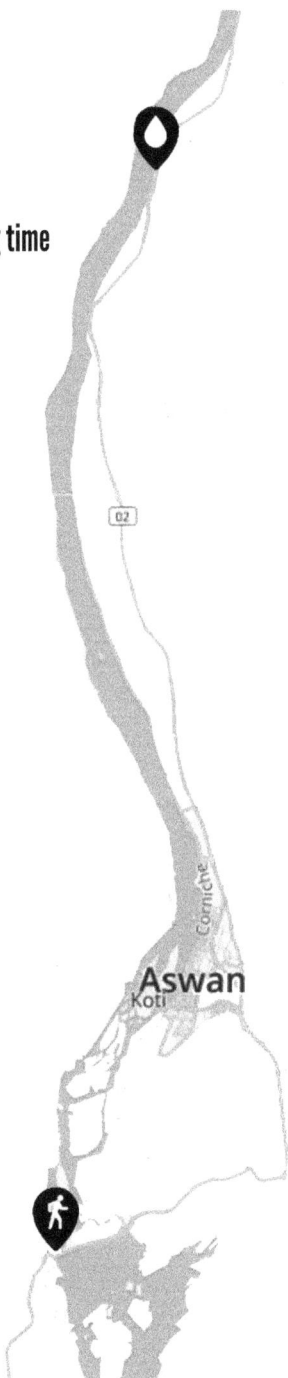

Day 2

AT FOUR-THIRTY AM I woke up. I felt better than the day before but still my left arm was hurting a bit and I knew that if my heart rate continued to be so high I would have to stop. I called Osama and Ahmed to wake them up, as we had agreed upon, and asked on the WhatsApp group if Younes was up too. He replied, "I am up, yes. You?" and I said, "I am up as well :p."

I went to the restaurant and Younes followed, Osama texting that he had woken but he wanted to continue sleeping and he thought that we should all sleep well and Ahmed saying that he also wanted to sleep but that he was getting ready and would be at the restaurant in ten minutes. I joked that we would be sleepwalking at this rate. Waking up in the morning was a daily struggle for Osama and Ahmed. Every day they came to breakfast late so we hit the road later than planned. This was frustrating for me and Younes, but we didn't talk about it in the beginning.

My heart rate was worrying me and so were my knees. I was telling Ahmed about my knee issue when Younes came over to ask what was wrong and we told him that it was nothing important. I hesitated to talk about this while Younes was around, not wanting him to think that I would be a burden on the team. After all, Ahmed and Osama have walked with me before the trip and they could see that it wasn't causing many problems. I didn't know how Younes felt about me joining the team, feeling that a group of three well-trained men would generally be faster and smoother than having a woman then join the team at the last minute.

Before heading to the cars I told Mohsen that I needed him to tape my knee. We checked several locations in the hotel to see where we could do this, but he didn't feel comfortable with any of them. Generally speaking, it is a part of Egyptian culture that a man and woman who are neither married nor related to one another will not be alone in an enclosed space together, especially when their interactions involve sensitive medical issues. A male doctor, for example, would always have a female doctor or nurse present when examining a female patient. It is a question of what is respectable and honorable, for both the man and the woman involved. So we found an empty hall and saw a maid passing by, so I asked her if she could stay with us for five minutes. I lay on the ground and rolled up my trouser legs. Mohsen asked me which color tape I wanted between green and purple, and I chose the purple though it wasn't going to show anyway.

I try to dress modestly. Arabic speakers might call me *muhajjaba* because I wear the hijab, though I don't like the classification, but modesty in dress is something that is important to me. Of course, how women choose to dress is a perennially controversial issue. When I studied in Leipzig, we were a group of forty-one, from six continents, twenty-three countries, and thirty-seven cities, and the fact that I wore the veil caused a stir in the first semester. I was told several times that I was oppressed. I argued that I came of my own free will to study in a western country. Did anyone really think I couldn't make a decision about how to dress? Still some of my female colleagues were skeptical. Then one day, my best friend came to visit me. She is also an Egyptian Muslim woman but she doesn't wear the veil. Only then did people start to believe me and see me differently.

In Egypt, when I first decided to dress modestly and to seal this decision by putting on the veil, some of my friends were shocked. One day I was wearing shorts and a crop top and the next I was wearing pants with a long, loose blouse and the veil. On the other hand, other people started criticizing me for not wearing my modest clothing "right." The sleeves were three quarter length, not covering my whole arm, for instance, or part of my hair was showing. But I wasn't concerned with such details, and at that point I told them, "Don't consider me *muhajjaba;* I just want to be modest." Everyone should be able to wear whatever he or she chooses, without classifications, and we should also be allowed to change our style when we want to.

Mohsen started taping from the back of my right knee and in less than ten minutes he was finished. I got up and rolled down my trouser legs, thanked Mohsen, and the cleaning lady and left to catch the guys.

I didn't expect to feel better that quickly, but already I found that walking was much smoother.

As we arrived at the cars, Osama said that he couldn't ride in the back again. I found Younes voluntarily sitting in the third row seat, while I took the front and only the two of us were in the car. I told him that this seat was not comfortable and he would get tired from the ride. He replied, "Someone has to compromise and I don't like complaints!" Osama, Ahmed, and Mohsen sat in the back seat. I took out my sunscreen and applied some on my face and hands; Ahmed also took some and in the end this became one of our rituals both in the car and in the middle of the day. While walking, I would take out the sunscreen and apply some and Ahmed would then take some from me and return it to my backpack. We drove to the point where we had stopped the day before, 12 km away from the hotel.

We assembled at the starting point, Younes counted three, two, one, and he and I started our trackers. We all started to walk. I was taking it slowly and constantly monitoring my heartbeat, which was elevated but not as much as the day before, so I relaxed a bit. Overall the start of the day was relaxed. We started with the previous day's scenery, the street a two-way road but with enough space for us to walk on it. The road curved and undulated as we came closer and closer to the Nile, until it was on our left with narrow green fields between us and the railway road on our right. Every now and then a train passed by, either following our direction or the opposite one, and their sounds accompanied us on the road.

But on this day I started to notice a problem. When the guys wanted to pee, they just had to find a tree and pee. Put simply, I couldn't do the same—I had to find somewhere hidden. While walking, we came across a huge field on our left containing a high-walled building without a ceiling. I went inside and Ahmed and Mohsen, who were walking with me then, waited for me.

We caught up with Younes and all walked for a while together until the videographer came and took some photos of us walking. Then the guys went ahead of us and I stopped with him for a while to take photos over a wall by the Nile that looked like a castle. He took a few shots of me over the wall then we walked rapidly to catch up with the guys. He told me that he was glad that he had had this opportunity to shoot such an important event and be with us for the twenty-four days of the challenge. Then he told me that he was working with us on a freelance basis and that, to do this, he had quit his full-time job. The problem was that the challenge had originally been scheduled to take place in November and was then postponed to January, so he had stayed all this time without a job. But he thought that it was worth it anyway. I told him that I was there, taking part in this challenge, through sheer luck and somehow it felt weird—he was more excited about it than I was, and he appreciated what I was doing more than I did. I couldn't grasp the importance of the challenge yet, and kept wondering—was he exaggerating?

When we reached the guys, Osama was sitting upset on the truck of the car and the others were surrounding him. Since the start of the day Osama had been acting weird; he walked alone all the time, striding ahead quickly. I inferred that he was upset that we were late and took it lightly, telling him that we had stopped for photos which unfortunately made him more irritable.

We continued our walk but we all were tired and hungry; in the middle of nowhere there was nowhere to eat, so we had to continue walking. It was coming up to noon and it was so hot that Younes told me I should wear a cap to avoid sunburn or sun stroke. I don't like how I look in a cap and my hesitant face must have spoken volumes. He told me that he had an extra hat but I replied that I had one of my own, taking it out of my bag. I didn't look so bad after all.

After some time, I was walking with Ahmed and Osama in the front and they started talking about Younes's endurance. It had been expected that he would arrive exhausted because just before the challenge he had been hiking abroad and after returning to Cairo he stayed less than a day before flying to Aswan. We had all assumed he must be deadly tired but he actually looked good and was more energetic than the other guys. Though sometimes he walked more slowly, when we rested and all took our shoes off, raising our legs to get the blood flow circulation moving, he didn't. Not only that—he didn't drink water at all during the walk, or so the guys said. We all had hiking backpacks with water bladders that we wore all the time, but Younes didn't and he encouraged us to leave them in the car to lighten our load. But I wanted my water, sun screen, power bank, wallet, and my pack of Fizz electrolytes[4] with me all the time.

I went back to Younes and asked him, "Younes, you don't drink water? It's hot and your body must need it."

He replied that he was not feeling thirsty and he wasn't sweating. I tried to argue that his body might still need it, especially given the afternoon heat, but when it came to his body Younes always had one answer: "I know my body very well." He never said this aggressively, but he was assertive.

We passed several very small villages on our way and mostly they looked very poor. The houses consisted of one or two floors, and some were without roofs, but I didn't see many people on the road. After 23 km, almost five hours of walking, we found a big "Daraw City welcomes you" sign. We entered a busy city with many trucks, that contrasted with the donkey carts and tricycles we had seen before. There were local coffee shops on the street and people sat on tables and chairs on the sidewalk, smoking shisha and drinking tea. They were mostly wearing *jilbab* and they had caramel colored skin and short black or white hair. The houses stood three or four floors high with red stones, all unpainted.

I was super tired but the name Daraw kept ringing in my ears, reminding me of a song, "wallah barrawa barrawa, wallah barrawa." I sang out loud "wallah darawa darawa." Osama gave me a look that seemed to say "crazy girl" and I laughed. He didn't, but he was just tired.

Daraw is considered a new city, almost seventy-five years old. Before becoming a city in its own right, it was a part of other cities. It has the oldest and largest camel market in the country, which used to be the most important camel market in all of Egypt and Sudan. In 2009 its population was more than 110,000 people living on almost 3000 acres of land. The main occupations of its inhabitants are farming and trading and the main crops produced sugar cane, dates, and wheat. It is said that the name Daraw comes from the name of the Pharaoh who

4 Electrolytes such as chloride, sodium, and potassium help replenish what was lost through sweat. Introducing electrolytes back into the body helps keep dehydration from occurring.

ruled that area back then; his name was Aw and Dar means house, so people used to say we are going to Dar Aw—the House of Aw.

The event management team had arranged for us to be seated in a cafeteria in Daraw and they were bringing us food from another place. We walked until we reached the cafeteria, which wasn't a usual one—at least to us. When we entered, we found a passageway in the middle and small seating areas on the right and left each covered from above with khayameya (a brightly patterned, traditional Egyptian cloth) which also separated the different seating areas. This provided shade from the strong sunlight of the afternoon. Younes, Samy, and Osama went into one of the seating areas, Ahmed into another, and the rest of the team spread out in different ones. I went into Younes's, Samy was attempting to sleep, so he took up a whole couch, but when he saw me he bent his knees and continued sleeping. Osama also made himself comfortable on the couch in front of me. I sat on the side of the couch, took off my shoes, and had a small talk with Younes about sportswear materials, then left to go change and pee.

I stood up—which is not always easy after a five hour walk—and went in the direction I saw other people heading, away from where we came in. I entered the huge tent I saw and asked about the toilet. The men I addressed there looked at me as if I was an alien who had just landed on their planet. One of the policemen who were ensuring our security was sitting with them and he stood up to show me the way. We went out of the tent and across the sandy earth, over to two mechanic shops with a toilet in the middle. There was a car being fixed just in front of the bathroom. It didn't look promising but I had to go anyway. I went inside and there was a small sink, filled with food and other detritus, followed by another door which led to the toilet. Entering, I found a *baladi* or "local" toilet, which is basically a hole in the ground. I felt relieved because baladi toilets are in many ways much cleaner than regular ones, as there is no touching in the process. I peed and changed into lighter clothes because it was much warmer than it had been in the morning, then returned to the cafeteria.

I found Samy and Osama sleeping so I went over to the seating area where Ahmed was resting. I made myself comfortable on one of the couches and he did the same on another. Then he asked Mohsen to come and massage his muscles and help him do some stretches. Mohsen instructed me to try to raise my legs and so I did.

Both Ahmed and I ordered lemon juice and Osama, waking, asked Mohsen to go to him as well to help stretch his legs. Then the food arrived and I asked Younes to join us. He opened his bag of food and found sauces falling out of the packs. I looked at what I had and discovered I had fewer sauces but rather rice, vegetables, and grilled chicken. Younes had meat with sauce but the look on his face showed that he was not satisfied. I asked him if he wanted to change but he said he was willing to eat what he had. Hamdy was passing by so I asked him if there was any more of the grilled meat; he asked me if we wanted to change and Younes affirmed. So Hamdy brought him another bag of food. Younes thanked me and came to sit by my side and, before long, Osama came to join us. After finishing our food, we lay down and started losing track of time. It was very warm and we lay there like turtles, stuck to one spot on our backs. Younes took charge, telling us that we needed to start getting ready. At this point, it was around three-thirty pm and two hours remained until sunset, while we still had 15 km ahead of us to complete that day. So we ordered coffee and left after twenty minutes.

As we hit the road, it was still busy and after almost an hour we found ourselves on a narrow two-way street, with factories to our left and fields to our right. The street was full of cargo cars and trucks, most of which had black emissions coming out of them. We were in Kom Umbu. In 2011, its population count was a little over 335,000 and it measured almost 3000 km². It is forty-four years older than Daraw. Sugar and cereal production are its main agricultural and economic activities, while its main source of pollution is the city's sugar factory, dating almost all the way back to when the city itself was established.

I put part of my headscarf over my mouth and nose and tried to walk quickly, hoping that the heavily-polluted part of the journey would end quickly. Younes was in front, accompanied by men from the Red Cross, then I followed with another Red Cross representative, and then finally Osama and Ahmed were at the back, where they seemed to have disappeared.

Members of the Red Cross from each governorate were joining our walk to perform basic first aid in case it was needed. They could choose to stay in their cars, which followed us on our journey, or to walk—and often many of them preferred to walk. Generally, they wanted to ensure that at least one person accompanied each of us. The team member who was my companion at this point was bony and of medium height; he was so thin as to actually look ill. He was complaining about his life, telling me that he loved to sleep and didn't really like doing anything else. It was only when someone needed help, he told me, that he would make an effort to help, but otherwise he doesn't have any aims in life. He didn't even like his studies, nor did he want a specific career. I was interested and eager to be a person he could potentially talk to, as we discussed his need to make a living and his need for a job. Volunteering, he told me, was great but if he continued simply as a volunteer he would need to rely on people's charity to live. I told him that since he liked helping people so much maybe this could be his career; he could work for an NGO that aimed to support people.

As he was getting tired, I told him to go and sit in the car for a while. He refused, saying he didn't want to leave me alone. I felt under pressure when he told me this. I didn't want to be the reason for him to be injured, especially because I really didn't feel that I needed anyone walking beside me all the time. I also felt a little frustrated that many of these Red Cross volunteers weren't physically ready to walk such distances, nor were their uniforms appropriate; they wore safety shoes that were so rigid that if a car ran over their feet they wouldn't feel the impact, and these shoes were very heavy. I decided to run to catch up with Younes so the Red Cross volunteer could rest, but I found that he continued to walk after us along with the other team members.

It was getting dark after walking that afternoon for ten kilometers, so Younes stopped to gather the team. We called Ahmed and learned that he was two kilometers away, which meant that he was twenty minutes behind us. Younes decided that we should stop for the day. We were a bit behind schedule but we knew by the time Ahmed would arrive, it would already be dark and Younes didn't think it was safe to walk in the dark. In the end it was better for all of us to call it a day. We stopped our trackers and I pinned our location on Google Maps and when Ahmed arrived we rode the cars back. This time, Mohsen went to ride in the support car, and, from now on, Mohamed, one of the drivers who had been hired by the event management team, and his car became mainly for the walkers, "the walker's car."

It had been a long day. We had walked 33 kilometers instead of the planned 38 because of the times we had stopped on the road and our long lunch break. On our ride back, I told the team that in future I would prefer if we had our lunch break at noon because it is the hottest time of the day, and that having the sun straight over our heads made me feel more tired than the walk. But they were all silent.

We arrived at the hotel. As we wanted to eat in a nearby place, to save time, sleep early, and wake up early, we went to a restaurant five minutes away. The four of us sat together and the support team sat next to us. We checked the menu and ordered soup, molokhia (a soup made of a leafy green vegetable, with chicken stock and lots of garlic), and grilled chicken or meat. The food was delicious.

After finishing, we were in the middle of a final talk when Hamdy informed us that, in the last three days of our trip, we would be staying at a hotel in Cairo. He thought that he was giving us good news, but to me it wasn't at all. We were going to enter Cairo, our final destination, by car before returning the following morning to where we had stopped the day before in order to walk, then once again we would be driven to the hotel . . . and this would go on for the last three days! I was upset because I wanted to enter Cairo on foot the first time, after our twenty-four days of effort, walking to reach the city.

When I expressed my feelings to the guys, Osama sharply replied, "Do you think that you will walk with us all the way or what?"

This statement felt so harsh to me. I knew that I wouldn't be able to walk the whole distance, but at least I was trying.

I answered quickly, "Even if not, at least I will be walking a little each day and I still want to enter on foot."

I was already not feeling very good. I was having difficulty standing and walking after such a long day, which marked the first time I had walked all this distance in one day. Quickly, the guys changed the subject and before long we were ready to leave.

I went to my room, took a shower, and went to bed, Osama's words still ringing in my ears. I started to cry, though I wasn't sure why I was so upset. Maybe it was because I had thought we would be having fun together, not pressuring each other. Or maybe the physical stress was making me more vulnerable. After ten minutes of feeling bad I decided that I wouldn't let these thoughts and feelings affect me and I would try to sleep to be able to wake up refreshed and on time.

Sleeping wasn't easy. Every time I was on the brink of falling asleep, I started to feel pain all over my legs. It didn't even come all at once; one part would start hurting considerably and then as it got a bit better, another part would start hurting. I remained in this discomfort for two hours, not knowing what to do or even how to lie. When I was on my side, my bottom knee couldn't handle the weight of my other knee, and when I was on my front, my ankles hurt. Finally I found that my best option was to lie still on my back, until all the pain faded away bit by bit and I fell asleep.

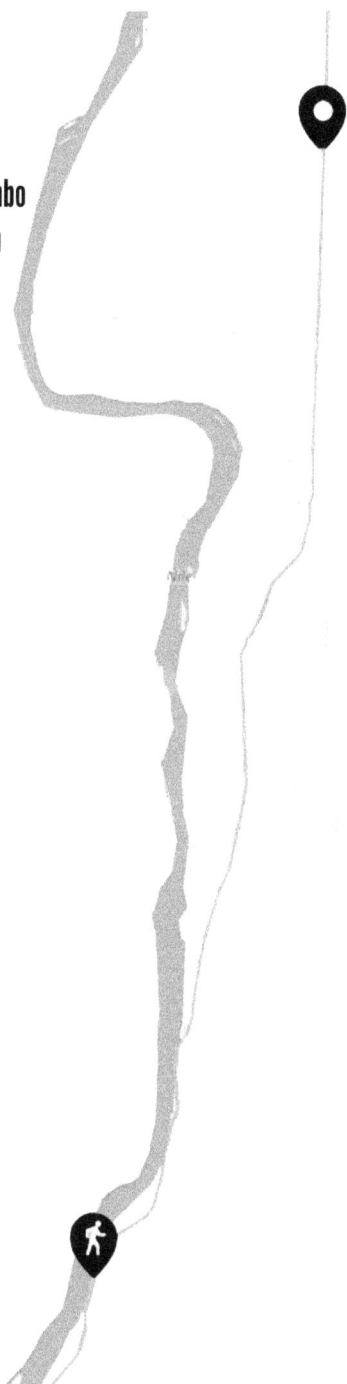

Day 2
ASWAN
Daraw, Kom Umbo
25km – 7h 35m

Day 3

I WOKE UP at four-thirty am. It was a new day but I wasn't feeling great because of the events of the previous day. I tried to get out of bed and I was amazed; I could stand up without pain! After the two hours of pain the day before, I had thought that I would have to rest for at least a day. But, miraculously, my body healed itself while sleeping. The previous day, Osama hadn't asked me to wake him up, so I was happy not to.

Younes was the first one at breakfast. This day I was fifteen minutes late and still I arrived before Ahmed and Osama. We were still staying in Aswan at the Helnan hotel, so we had to drive 45 km to reach the starting point of our walk that day, an hour's drive because of the narrow Agricultural Road. We were supposed to leave the hotel at five-thirty am, but we ended up departing around six, reaching our starting point at seven.

Younes sat in the front seat and the other three of us in the back, with Osama on one side, Ahmed in the middle and me behind Younes. On our way, Ahmed told me that they were very glad that I had joined them on the adventure, Younes agreed vehemently and then Osama too said, "yes we are." I knew that Ahmed was trying to ease the damage that was done over dinner the previous night and the truth was, it *did* make me feel better. At least I knew they cared enough to try to make me feel good. I didn't understand what was happening with Osama. He was so different than how he had been before we arrived in Aswan.

Having reached our starting point, I stood behind one of the car doors, hiding from the street to put on the strap that would measure my heart rate. The guys were at the back, putting their shoes on and while we were all getting ready, Osama started walking on his own. Then as usual, we stood at the starting point, Younes counted down three, two, one and we started our tracking devices: GO!

We were in sugarcane world, walking along a narrow street with fields of tall sugarcane trees to our right and left. There were many cars loading sugarcane all the way to Luxor, offering it free of charge to passersby. Everyone we saw in the street was running over to the cars, grabbing one or two sticks of sugarcane and peeling them, throwing away the outer layer, and chewing the rest. Some of the sugarcane had fallen on the ground and been run over by passing cars, so the streets were sticky. At each step, we felt our shoes were glued to the ground. Because sugarcane trees are high and clustered together, I didn't have any problems finding somewhere to pee then. In fact, I found them the best place to hide.

It was a beautiful walk, with canals that crossed under the road every now and then. Younes was playing music on his loud speakers. Ahmed was walking in front, then Younes, then me, and Osama was a little behind me—all of us walking in a row. Younes was dancing in time with the music, and so was I, so I walked to his side and told him, "We need to have dancing moves for the trip."

"I just move with the music," he answered, "I don't have specific moves."

We smiled and continued walking in a row.

On the road there were always dogs in front of the fields, guarding them. Almost each field had a dog or two barking when we passed by. When we were walking quietly I answered the dogs. Osama had looks of disbelieve to me, he was like, "What are you doing?"

"Talking to the dogs in their own language."

"So what would you do with cats?"

"I meow!"

"And birds?"

"I tweet!"

"And you bray with donkeys?"

"I would if I could . . ."

After 10 km of a beautiful walk connecting with the nature I had to pee again, but this time the fields didn't have enough trees to hide me. I kept walking, waiting for a place to appear where I could pee. Opening Google Maps, I found a gas station nearby, but when I reached it, the station was under renovation. I continued walking for around an hour, holding it in and hoping. Finally, after four kilometers, a village appeared and I knew that each village had a train station. The guys stopped for a short break while I ran to the station and found a baladi toilet.

When I came back, Younes asked me to tell them when I was going to pee because they didn't want me to disappear suddenly.

I was going to argue with him but then I looked at him and muttered, "Okay."

He continued, "You know we may not be able to reach you over the phone," and it was as if he was answering my inner voice and understood my frustration.

After a ten minute break, we resumed our walk. Samy from the event management company came to walk with us. He is a tall man and had some extra weight that he wanted to lose. He walks quickly and I started to walk with him at the front. Here I observed that he listened to music fifty percent of the time, talked to his girlfriend thirty percent of the time and, in the remaining time, we talked. He was the youngest of three brothers. He told me that they used to tease him when he was younger and that he would tease them back. I discovered that teasing, in their book, meant hitting each other until they broke one another's arms. But this, he assured me, was when they were young and he turned out to be a warm and kind man after all. I didn't mind that he was listening to music most of the time, as I was also listening either to music or stories in German. Before starting the challenge, I had thought that being on the road for twenty-four days would give me the time to learn some new things, so I decided to improve my German. Because of this, I was listening to German stories for at least two hours on most days.

We left the village, Kalabsh, and walked through the fields for a while before entering a new village, Al Kajoj. As we entered this village, we found small houses stretching uphill on our right and houses on the left with fields behind them. It was calm with men and children in the street on foot or riding carts or tricycles while women, it seemed, stayed at home because they didn't appear in front of strangers unless they were fully covered and even then it was only when they had to.

Some of the village children were riding a tricycle and approaching us from behind. They must have seen the rest of the team by the time they reached me and Samy, because we were at the front, but strangely when they saw our backs they threw a rock at us which hit my right shoulder. I looked at Samy but he hadn't even noticed the incident so I took a deep breath and decided not to get upset.

After a while we wanted a short break. We stopped to wait for the rest of the team, who were right behind us. Younes started to ask if there was a cafeteria nearby but the man he had approached insisted that we go to his place for tea instead.

All along our way, most people we saw invited us for tea but of course we couldn't accept every invitation because we needed to continue the walk. We were very happy to go to this man's house, however. Houses in this particular village in Upper Egypt have small yards in front of them, with long wooden seats outside where the men sit, while the women are inside. I sat with the team outside; feeling tired I took my shoes off, but couldn't make myself very comfortable.

The man of the house came over and asked me, "Do you want to sit with the ladies inside?"

"Thanks, I am okay," I answered. I thought that he was suggesting this so that I would be more comfortable.

Younes was sitting beside me and he whispered, "Go inside."

I was numb for few seconds. I hadn't expected that from him.

Then the man asked me again, "Do you want to sit inside with the ladies?"

Younes whispered to me again to go inside.

I understood this time that this wasn't a question; it was more of an instruction for me to go inside. I stood up and the man showed me inside.

When I entered through the wooden door I found a corridor ahead of me, with a room on the left and, at the end of the corridor, an open-air area. The houses, both in these villages in particular and as a general trend in Islamic architecture, are built to allow the outside in. The open-air yard in the middle served as the main entrance for light and air, and all the rooms were situated around the yard. The purpose of this design is to ensure privacy for the tenants, with the windows of the rooms looking over the inside yard and not overseeing the streets and neighbors.

A woman came and invited me to enter, steering me towards the room on the left. It was a small room with two sofas and a chair. She brought her wedding album to show me and I went over to sit by her side, at this point glad of having gone inside because my feet did hurt and I wanted to take off my socks as well, and to raise my feet a bit. The woman was wearing a tight black jilbab and a colored headscarf. She was newly married to the nephew of the house owner. His parents had passed away and he lived with his aunt.

In the villages in Upper Egypt, families live together and, when the men of the family marry, their brides go to live with them in the family house. This woman was newly arrived in the house but the village was small and so everyone was familiar with everyone and everything in the village. In the album, I could see the bride and groom having henna drawings on their hands and palms. The groom wore black leather gloves covering only the top of his fingers, and that was to avoid the evil eye, she told me.

We talked a bit about life in the village for her as a newlywed. Her main chore was feeding her husband and her main problem was that he needed to have a different meal for dinner than for lunch, so she had to cook twice a day. For the rest of the day she would spend her time watching TV. She was an avid fan of Arabic, Turkish, and Indian TV series.

I asked if I could use the toilet, which was outside on the left. I showed myself out and discovered that it was a baladi toilet. I had a problem that day; I was experiencing chafing so I was in pain. The day before, I had seen the guys talking together in a way that seemed somehow secretive. Now I understood that they had been getting chafing after the first day's walk, and they were discussing how to deal with it. But they were embarrassed to talk about it in front of me. I took my time, not ready to reemerge until I was feeling a bit better. I was using water to calm the chafed skin a bit and I wanted to air the whole area as well. After five minutes I went back to the room.

The aunt had made us tea and came to sit with us. She was in her seventies, dressed in a loose, black jilbab and a big black headscarf. Though we were all quiet initially as she came to sit with us, gradually the family started teasing each other and laughing. I didn't understand most of the words, however; they talked in a strange dialect to me. Then the aunt asked what had brought me there and I told her that we were walking from Aswan to Cairo.

She asked me the question I had been afraid of her asking: "Are you alone with three men?"

"Yes," I answered, "but there is a team also with us to offer support."

I was doing something that was totally foreign to the culture of my hostess. They can't sit with men they are not closely connected or related to and they mostly have to speak to them from behind a door. For a woman to walk with three men for twenty-four days without any of them being her husband or a relative would be considered a scandal. The aunt was silent for a moment then looked at me and asked if I was married. I said that I wasn't.

As she smiled, she told me, "When you get married, you won't be able to do any of these things."

I answered, smiling, "Maybe he will also be an athlete and we will do these things together."

She thought for a moment, clearly wondering how to break the news to me. Then she said, "You will have to take care of your house and your husband's problems, and then you will get pregnant and you will have to stay with your children." Then she laughed. "I just don't want you to get a shock."

I laughed as well and found that I really didn't want to debate any more.

The man of the house appeared and I heard his voice from behind the door, telling me that the guys wanted to leave. So I excused myself, thanked my hostess, and her companions for the tea, put on my socks and shoes, and left. I was glad to see the guys. I had enjoyed the talk inside but I also wanted to know what they had been doing. We resumed our walk.

Younes was quick to tell me that he had been a little forceful when encouraging me to go inside because that was the custom here.

"Yes, I understand that now, but at first I thought the man was suggesting for me to go inside—not asking or telling me to go inside," I answered. "What have you been doing?"

"Nothing much," he answered. "We had tea, twice, and he wanted us to stay for food but we kept telling him that we couldn't do that, because we had to hit the road soon. He didn't want to accept this response, so we had to insist on leaving."

"What was it like inside?" he asked, so I told him everything in detail before Samy came to me asking the same question. I answered him in detail as well.

After some time, we had walked 18 km, taking almost five hours to cover this distance, including two small rests. It was eleven-thirty and the sun was over our heads. I was getting tired of the sun and my feet were hurting. I told Ahmed that we would need to rest soon. Younes overheard us and came and asked me if I could keep walking until we reached the 25 km mark. He looked at me with his head lowered, as if he was peering at me over a pair of glasses but without actually having glasses on. I felt that I had no options. He was more telling than asking me. And the feeling that I was extraneous to the whole activity and that maybe they would feel that if I couldn't continue then I should rest, and not continue, made me stressed and anxious. I wasn't happy about it but I told him that I could keep going.

We kept walking, becoming more and more tired. It was really hot that day. I was counting each kilometer and walking as fast as I could to finish the misery as quickly as possible. Furthermore, I was drinking a lot of water because of the heat, so I needed to pee again. I looked for a place where I could stop, but the fields were so exposed. I kept holding it in until I coughed and peed a little in my pants. I felt worried, and awful. Then I found a mosque, so, to my relief, I was able to enter and change.

After another hour and a half we had completed the 25 km but we found ourselves virtually in the middle of nowhere. There was a mountain on our right and fields with tall trees to our left gave a bit of shade on the street. Ahmed called Hamdy to see where we could have our lunch break and was told that there was a gas station ten minutes away. So it was decided that we walk for ten more minutes. Ahmed, who looked so tired as well, came to walk at the front and then started running. We all gravitated to the left side of the street, to get some shade from the trees. And the ten minutes turned out to be another hour. The gas station was five kilometers away, which was only ten minutes by car but sixty minutes on foot!

Beside the station was a cafeteria and, in front of this, a grassy area. I quickly went to look for the nearest tree to rest under. I took off my shoes and lay down on the ground, feeling my face burning red from the heat. Mohsen came to check on me.

"Are you all right?" he asked.

"No," I answered.

I didn't even have the ability to pretend that I was fine. He sat beside me, full of concern and empathy. I drank some water and raised my legs, entirely focused on my physical well-being. It was only then that I started noticing the things around me.

I saw the cafeteria—which was full of men—then I saw Younes, who was sitting straight up on a chair with his shoes on, still wearing his sunglasses and cap. I don't know what he was thinking, but he stood up, approached me, and looked down at me lying on the ground.

"Up to now, we've walked 30 kilometers, which is equal to the distance we covered yesterday, and it's still the middle of the day," he said, before leaving.

I had mixed thoughts. I knew that he wanted to tell me that this was big progress, but the way his words came out didn't give that sense. Still, I was comforted. I started feeling better, so I looked for Osama and Ahmed and found them lying on their backs on another part of the grass. Frankly, it was a good feeling to know that I was not alone in this, being tormented.

The food had arrived, I went to wash up and found Younes sitting with the videographer and the social media rep. I joined them and found that they were talking about what exactly the social media company did. I remained quiet; I didn't have enough energy for my brain to work and couldn't even focus on what they were saying. But I found myself wondering how Younes could find something to engage and interest him in every person he talked to. Every day, people from the Red Cross would join us and he would ask questions about the geography of the area, the agricultural crops, the canals, the tribes, and communities living in each village. And whenever he met someone new from the same area, he didn't get bored of having the same conversations. The first day the Red Cross team started walking with us he was friendly and talkative, but always maintained his personal space. But each day or each half day he was able to mingle with people more closely. His Arabic wasn't very good, but he was very attentive to what people said and would then repeat it, so he had, in a way, learned the language better on the road. Although Arabic is our mother tongue in Egypt, many wealthier Egyptians study at international schools, where speaking English is prioritized over speaking Arabic.

Osama had appeared while we were in the middle of having lunch. He sat alone on another table to eat. Ahmed then appeared after the rest of us had finished our food and started eating. He told us that he had been away having a physiotherapy session. Younes started to say that we would need to get going soon, but in a way Osama and Ahmed were in a different world. I think they were more tired than I was. We ordered coffee and I went to sit by Ahmed as we drank it. Younes was talking on the phone and Osama was doing some stretches with Mohsen.

Ahmed was worried about the call that Younes was having and asked me, "Do you think it's a personal call or is he on the phone with our main sponsors?"

I told him that really didn't concern me and asked, "Why are you worried?"

The main sponsors were planning to publish a press release about the walking challenge and they didn't want to include our names. Younes was upset about this; after all, the challenge had been his idea so he needed credit and acknowledgment of the effort we had put into it, and he told us several times that we needed to speak up as well, for our rights to be respected. From my side, I wasn't planning to do the entire walk so it didn't make sense that I would speak out about this issue. So Younes had decided to talk to the press to ensure that his own press release was published, and now it seemed that Ahmed was worried that Younes would not include his name.

I told Ahmed that I didn't see anything bad about Younes and that, on the contrary, he had behaved really well with everyone.

Ahmed nodded his agreement. "But his actions will show the truth about his ethics—he wouldn't have been able to do it without me."

"Sure," I answered, "but if you are so eager to have your name written in the press release then you should talk with the main sponsors."

"Why put effort in a war that someone else is fighting?" he replied.

We were finally all ready to go and Mohsen asked me if I needed anything. I told him that I only needed tape to put on my leg, just above my ankle, because the friction from my shoes was causing me pain. Osama asked how I was feeling and I gave a positive answer. He seemed astonished, but I didn't care. There were ten kilometers left for us to complete that day, it was after three pm and we wanted to finish before it started to get dark, which would usually be at around five pm.

The next ten kilometers led us uphill along a narrow, curving road between two mountains. The terrain was majestic and it was exhilarating to be walking there, yet so tiring. For two hours we walked in the late afternoon light, between rock-covered mountains that glowed yellow and orange, then it started to get dark and we lost mobile network coverage. With only three kilometers to go, I found that the guys started running to finish quickly. I knew that I could not do that; my feet were already hurting a lot and I was sure that when the others had finished the three kilometers they would wait for me anyway.

When we finished I was extremely excited, telling Ahmed, "This is my first time to walk 40 kilometers ever!" I told him this because of my overwhelming feeling of gratitude towards him for telling me about the adventure in the first place.

I pinned the location, we rode back in the cars and I found myself vividly remembering the first walk I undertook to prepare for the challenge. On that day, I went with Ahmed to walk early in the morning, thinking that the plan was to walk around 8 km. After completing the first 2 km, I felt that I could walk another three. After 4 km I was getting tired, but I knew I could walk two more. We had ended up walking 24 km in four hours, and of course I walked like a penguin for two days afterwards. Remembering this, a huge smile broke out on my face, then I fell asleep.

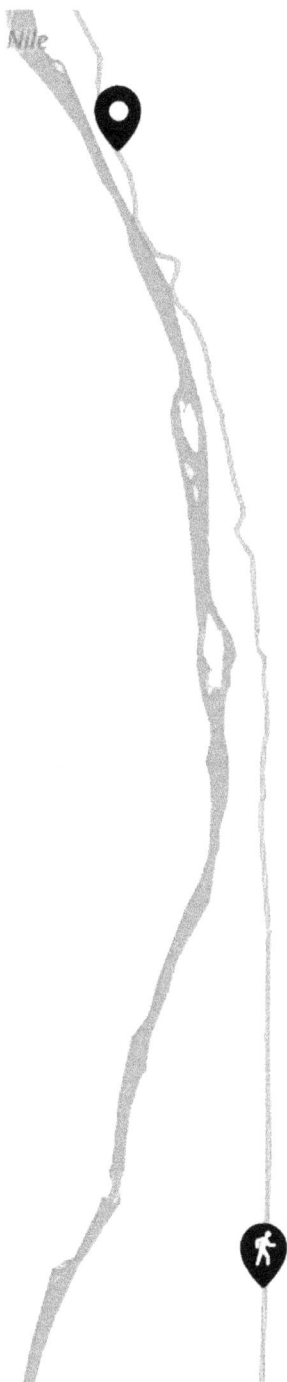

Day 3
ASWAN
Kalabsh, Al Kajoj
40km – 8h 35m

Nile

Day 4

I WOKE UP at four-thirty am, prepared my bags, and was ready to go. The previous day, we had learned that the event management company had hired a new employee, Sally. We didn't know exactly what she was here to do, but last night she had texted, reminding us to pack our bags to be ready to check out of the hotel in the morning before leaving for the walk and asking if we needed anything from the city center. Younes had asked for four hats, which he wanted us to wear, with the Egyptian flag on them. He had wanted to go to the bazaar for that but there wasn't enough time. I had asked for Brufen 400, a medication containing Ibuprofen. My period was due to come soon and I was worried that the flow might be high or that I would be in a lot of pain or lose energy. I had Googled possible solutions and found out that Ibuprofen is anti-inflammatory, reducing pain and helping to control the period flow.

The day before, I had slept in the car for almost two hours as we drove the 86 km we had covered on foot so far, to reach the location of the hotel around nine pm. Osama, Ahmed, and I decided to have dinner in our rooms because we were so tired and we needed enough time to sleep. Ahmed and Osama asked Mohsen to go to their rooms, while I packed my bags and went to bed. Younes always wanted to do something after the walk, so he went to eat in the restaurant. At eleven I was woken up by a knock on the door and the appearance of food. It was delicious fish, with vegetables and rice. I ate a bit and returned to bed.

In the morning, I went to the restaurant at 5:45. Not everyone was there. We left around seven am and drove for two and a half hours to reach our starting point, between the mountains. It was a downhill walk and I was with Samy and Younes. We didn't talk much. Younes had music playing through his loudspeakers. His playlist had one artist: Avicii. I didn't know him before the trip, but had started to memorize his songs by now. It created a nice atmosphere, especially because we weren't always in the mood for talking, finding that we were either tired, or that it was still too early for deep conversations, or that the sun was burning our heads, or we had been talking with people from the Red Cross for so long that we were tired of talking. Or at least this is how I felt. I also liked having the opportunity to listen to German stories when I could.

So we just walked, listening to music, and Samy and I were trying to snap our fingers to the beat of the song. So Avicii started singing wondering if his brother still believes in him and if his sister still believes in love then he continues that in hard times there is nothing he wouldn't do for his siblings, Then we would snap our finger thrice after each stanza.

We passed through very nice scenery: a canal intersecting with the street, lined with palm trees on either side, and their reflections in the water. We stopped to take some photos, then took a couple of photos of Younes. He wanted to be at the center of each photo because he likes symmetrical photos. But when he was in the middle he hid the canal, so I took an asymmetrical photo of him and made the background symmetrical. He wasn't very pleased at me breaking his golden rule.

Osama was walking behind the rest of us and arrived while we were taking photos. "So everyone has taken the same photo or is anyone missing?" he asked sarcastically.

"No, there are a few spaces left!" I replied, teasing him. But he continued walking ahead of us, grumpy.

Younes and I continued walking. I asked him, "Why is it that you love Egypt so much? What made you so passionate about Egypt?"

"I was raised in a house of politicians, or people working closely with the government," he said.

His grandfather on his mother's side, it turned out, was close to the president of his time, Gamal Abdel Nasser, and his family on his father's side have always been politicians and ministers.

"In our house, there are always discussions about the political situation, what's best for the country, how special our country is, and so on."

"So the name of Egypt is repeated in your house many times a day," I said.

"Exactly," he replied.

Students from the Faculty of Physical Education in Aswan City had arrived to join our walk. There were around thirty girls and forty boys. I high-fived the girls and walked with them, and the guys went over to walk with the boys. The girls were wearing makeup, which I thought was unnecessary for the walk.

When I told them this, they answered me "We don't like going out without makeup. Even at university, makeup is forbidden but we still wear it."

This was a total surprise for me; I had thought that in Aswan I would find the girls not merely more conservative than in Cairo, but much more conservative than they actually were. They were even flirting with Osama so he had to literally run away from them! He started running so that they wouldn't catch him.

Things between me and Osama were gradually getting better. We didn't speak often, asking one another only how we were feeling in the mornings, or during the breaks. Occasionally we would have small, jokey exchanges, and the tension was breaking slowly. After two hours walking with the athletes, he asked me how I was doing. I told him that I was a bit stressed out because of walking with the girls, who were very competitive. Each wanted to be walking at the front and those who found themselves there often walked too quickly, to maintain their position, so others couldn't keep up. I had to try to control the situation by being at the front myself and slowing down, so no one would be left behind.

I asked him how it was going with the guys. He told me that everything was ok, but that he was also stressed out because he had to run from the girls and two of them had continued to chase him for a while until they gave up. We laughed at how unusual this situation was; usually it seems that it's the guys who are the ones chasing. By then it was lunch time and we went to a restaurant in the city, Edfu, in the middle of Aswan governorate.

This was our first time to eat lunch at a proper restaurant since our journey began and afterwards we took the car to return to the start line. Ahmed was sitting in the front, I was behind him and then Younes and Osama sat beside the window, behind the driver's seat.

Osama asked me, "Why don't you sit in the front instead?"

"Am I making you uncomfortable?" I asked.

"No," he replied, but I wasn't sure I believed him.

For the past two days, he had repeatedly told me to go and sit in the front. I knew of course that the guys could relax more and make themselves more comfortable without me beside them, but I also couldn't ask anyone to leave the front seat for me. And sometimes our car rides were short, so there was no need for all this fuss. But it seemed that Osama was very aware of my presence, even if I wasn't beside him. Or maybe he thought that it would really be better for me, so the gentleman in him wanted to make sure that the lady was comfortable. Younes realized what was happening, as did Ahmed, so in the end the three of them left the front seat for me when the four of us rode together. Sometimes Osama preferred to go with the support team in their car.

We returned to the start line to resume the walk. Though we still had 20 km to walk, it was getting late and we ended up walking only ten. I walked at the front and Osama was just behind me. Then we arrived at a turning and I didn't know the way, so Osama stepped forward to be at the front and we turned left. We walked companionably, but we were both together and not. When he slowed down I would come to the front, then he would walk faster and walk by my side, before again overtaking me, and so on.

Then we turned right into a busy area. There were teenagers hanging around who weren't so nice. They made some flirtatious comments to me, but no one came close. Osama looked at me and said, "Why don't you go to the back and walk with the others? Or you don't mind these guys flirting?"

"No I can handle it," I said quickly, "and they are not saying anything offensive."

And you are here beside me, I was thinking, but this I kept to myself and stepped forward a little.

After we finished that day we drove to Luxor, to a new city and a new hotel. The idea of walking the whole distance still seemed farfetched when I thought about it. Yes, we had walked more than 120 km and I had never imagined doing this, but the total distance of 938 km was almost eight times what we had already walked, so I still had my doubts, especially as I was going to get my period soon.

We reached Luxor at night, pulling up to the Jolie Ville hotel. It was huge; the hotel was an island with several swimming pools overlooking the Nile, and it had a zoo and several restaurants. We left our luggage in the lobby and went to the restaurant, a five minute walk away. It had an open buffet, and I remember eating a strawberry jelly for dessert, because jelly is good for the knees.

Younes said that he didn't eat sweet things. We started debating what constituted sweet food, with me asking if he considered jelly to be sweet. He answered that it has a lot of sugar in it. I found it difficult to believe he didn't eat any of the delicious desserts we have in Egypt, telling him incredulously that basbousa is sweet and kanafeh is sweet.

Then Hamdy interjected, "You are sweet."

His comment made me uncomfortable, but I didn't want it to show, so I tried to deflect it by looking at the guys and asking them, "Do you hear the nice words?" I was jokingly implying that I never heard a nice word from any of them, but trying to do it in a way that took the focus off Hamdy and his words.

We went back to the lobby very tired. I was barely able to carry my legs or my legs to carry me, and we had to wait for a shuttle bus to take us to our rooms. When it arrived, the driver got out and we waited for another ten long minutes for him to return and the bus to move. Finally, we arrived in the area where our rooms could be found, and each searched for their own. I entered mine, opened my bag, and got out the pajamas, had a shower and went to bed with uneasy feelings about the coming days.

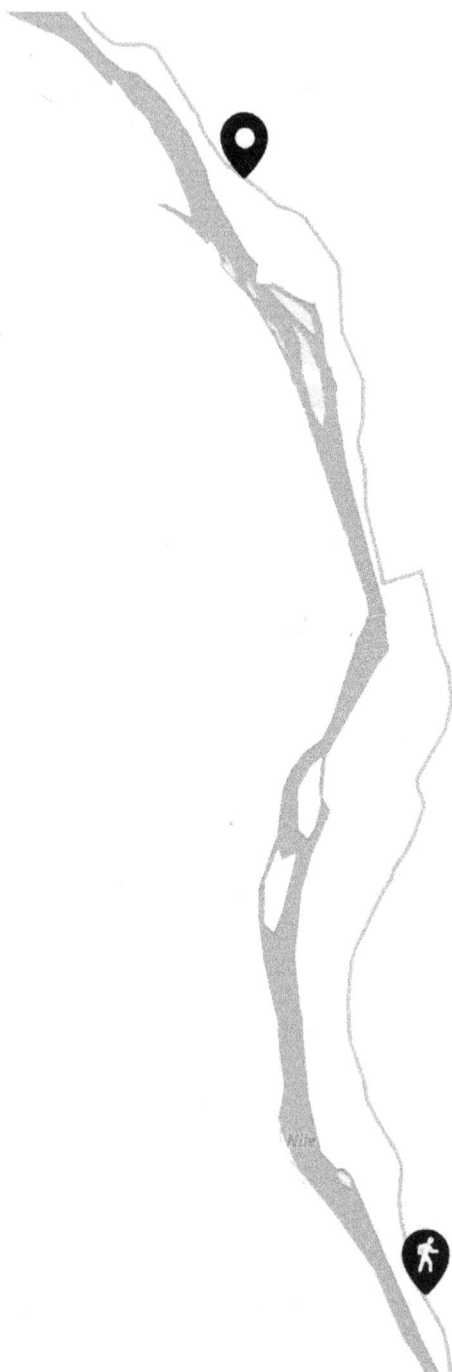

**Day 4
ASWAN**
Edfu
29km – 6h 25m

Day 5

THIS WAS A new day. Of course, every day is a new day but today many things were going to change, though I had no way of knowing this. I woke up at four-thirty am and got dressed as usual. By then, I had a system. I put on an undershirt, then a shirt, then another slightly warmer sports shirt, then a jacket. On the bottom, I wore only trousers and, on colder days, shorts underneath. On my feet, I wore my Crocs and carried proper hiking shoes with me to put on at the start point, and then I carried an extra bag with everything I mentioned inside as a backup.

The previous night had been one of those where I couldn't sleep immediately, because of the pain. Actually it was hard for me to even reach the shower. At first, I couldn't stand but I knew that after a hot shower I would feel better. This was true, but still I didn't feel well enough to sleep like a baby. After two hours of pain, I decided to take a painkiller and was so glad to have Brufen. I took one pill and went to sleep.

At five I reached the restaurant, still in the dark and cold. I was the first to arrive and ordered coffee, waiting, but after ten minutes no one else had appeared. We had to walk 42 km that day and had a long ride to reach the start point. We needed to move early.

The previous day, Osama had asked that someone wake him up. I had tried to call him in his room but there was no reply. The first to show up was Younes, with Hamdy. They had got lost, which had made them late. We sat at a table in the middle of the restaurant, started our breakfast, and waited for Ahmed and Osama to arrive. Ahmed appeared half an hour late and Osama fifteen minutes later, with both seeming as though they didn't care that they were late. They got their breakfast and started eating.

Osama asked, "Did any of you have a problem with your room?"

"Yes, it is too big," I answered.

"Yeah, I can see the door when I am in bed," Ahmed answered.

We all looked at him waiting for an explanation. It turns out that Ahmed doesn't like to see the door of the room when he is in bed, but he found that there was a curtain that he could pull across to cover it, so his problem was solved.

Then Younes looked at me and told me, "But, yeah, the room is very big; everything is scattered in different places."

"Exactly," I answered.

Osama looked at us incredulously, not believing that we could see these things as problems. I smiled inwardly.

Then Osama asked, "Did any of you find cockroaches in the bathroom?"

Younes answered that he had because they come out of the floor drain, so he had put a basket over it. Our rooms were on the ground floor and overlooking a garden. Osama said that he had found many cockroaches in the bathroom so he had stayed awake killing them for a while, then when he was too tired to continue he closed the bathroom door and slept.

When we finally finished breakfast we went over to the cars. Younes and I were trying not to show our irritation at always being kept waiting, and always starting our walks late. I was able to keep my cool because I saw that Younes kept his. We reached our starting point at seven-thirty. Just like every day, we prepared ourselves for the walk. We put our shoes on, I wore my heart rate strap, took my bag and headed to the start line. On this day, I did everything quickly because I wanted to pee, so I told the guys that I would walk ahead of them quickly to find a place to pee and would wait for them. There was a village 400 meters away and it was on our way. So I walked quickly and when I reached the village, I found that the road was narrow and full of buildings. I saw a hospital on my left, so I crossed the street, went inside and asked the receptionist if I could use the bathroom. He told me to go straight ahead and I would find it on the right. I showed myself there. When I came back to leave, the receptionist asked me where I was coming from. I suppose his curiosity was piqued, because the odds of a woman entering this hospital on the agricultural road to pee, and coming without male company or a car, were so slim in this village. I told him that I had come on foot from Aswan and he was stunned. He asked if I was alone and I told him that there were three men with me. As I left the hospital, I saw Osama and Younes crossing the road. They raised their hands in greeting to the man and we left.

On this day, Osama walked with Younes most of the time and Ahmed was at the back. He had been texting and making calls most of the day, ever since we arrived in the car, so we hadn't had many conversations with him and he didn't engage with us much. He walked either ahead of us all or at the very back. I listened to my German stories for two hours continuously, walking ahead of the others but regularly checking behind me to make sure that the guys were within my field of vision.

The road curved, and sometimes we could see the Nile to our left and at other times only green fields. On our right, there was a huge mountain that loomed over us. I was enjoying the road, then I found a place to rest that was built out of mud and was like an arch. Inside, there were a built-in seat on the right and another on the left, beside the wall. In the middle were clay water vessels. The atmosphere inside was great. I rested for a while and five minutes later Osama arrived. He asked me if I was okay and I told him that I was waiting for them. He sat with me, then Younes arrived. We rested a bit, then the guys went searching for a place to pee.

We found caves in the mountain far away and we wanted to go and explore them, but it would have taken at least an hour, so reluctantly we decided to skip it. Later we found out that this was the remains of a temple, named Elkab, dating from the Early Dynastic period (3100–2686 BC) to the Ptolemaic Kingdom (332–30 BC).

As we resumed our walk, we saw smaller caves in the mountains above, which were part of ElKab area. Younes and I were both interested in hiking to them. They were much smaller than the caves that were far away but we were still glad that we would be able to have an impression of the whole. We started exploring the area a little, with Osama and then Ahmed following us. We were always aware of the time, so we did everything quickly. We took a few photos, then went down and continued our walk.

Younes, Osama, and I were ahead and Ahmed was at the back. We found two men wearing *jilbab* and riding donkeys, carrying sugarcane. We greeted them and they asked us what we were doing. We told them our story as we walked along beside them. One of them told us, "If you hadn't decided to do this walk, we wouldn't have met you." They wanted to give us sugarcane, but we were in a hurry, so we took a picture with them and left.

This was a nice day, with good weather and not much tension in the air. After we had walked for 12 km, taking two and a half hours, Hamdy told us that we had to go to a youth center. They were assembled and waiting for us, so they could learn more about the challenge. We joined them in playing treasure hunt: the young people had been divided into teams, with each team trying to find the treasure by solving clues. Each of us joined one of the teams and helped them a bit.

The clues were all related to the disadvantages of child marriage, which is an unfortunate reality of life in this part of Egypt. The problem in these areas is that, culturally, men occupy a very dominant position and it is commonly accepted that they command women in what to do. The preponderance of child marriage and the lack of family planning negatively and seriously affect the women, from the time they are girls, limiting their aspirations in life.

I was with a team of girls, and after finding the treasure we celebrated. I told them that I had walked from Aswan and that the guys and I would continue walking to Cairo. They were astonished, and asked me why I was doing this. I replied that I wanted to challenge myself, and that I was amazed that I had been able to walk the full distance with the guys over the past four days. I explained how this had helped me realize that we, as women, are strong and that we have great abilities. I asked them if they played sports and they answered in the negative. We talked about the importance of sports, and all kinds of knowledge, for them to have confidence in their abilities and to love themselves. One of the girls then asked, laughing, "And what about cooking?" We all laughed, but I knew she was serious. I told her that we can learn how to cook, play sports, and read about astronomy if we want.

They asked me how I could do the entire walk. I answered that I have always played sports, ever since I was a child, and that I practiced artistic gymnastics for seven years. They didn't know what this was, so I showed them a movement: the cartwheel. They were amused; it was like a circus show for them and they wanted to take a photo with me. After we said our goodbyes, while I was walking away, one of the girls called after me, and told me that she didn't want me to publish the photos. For many girls and women from particularly modest backgrounds in Egypt, they don't want their image to be available in a public space, like any form of social media, where it could be seen by men they do not know. Because of this, some girls will put on their Facebook profiles an image of a flower or a butterfly, and even use a nickname, like the *flower of hope* or *bird of paradise,* to hide their identities.

We went to have lunch at the same place as we had the day before. The waiter there didn't like us very much because Osama and Ahmed had been a bit mean to him the day before. They kept asking him questions, then laughed when he answered. Osama had been playing a game because he had a theory that people in Edfu would never directly admit to not knowing the answer to a question they were asked. So he kept asking people how Edfu had got its name. Everyone gave a different answer. One person said that it was named Edfu after a scholar called Al Edfawy. Another had said that it was because, when there was a war, it had been fought from here, so the place was called Edfu. It didn't make any sense to us when we first heard it, but after researching I found out that Edfu stood on the southern border of Egypt at the beginning of Egyptian recorded history. And its name comes from its original situation as a frontier settlement. It means "place of the throne."

Osama found these answers very funny, so he would laugh out loud whenever he heard one. Ahmed knew what he was doing, so he was joining him in the fun. I didn't understand what was going on and could see that Younes had a serious look on his face. In all the twenty-four days we were together, I never saw Younes make fun of anyone. On the contrary, he was respectful to everyone. So, I don't know whether he was ignorant of what they were doing, like me, or had just decided that he would not join in their actions.

After lunch, I found that my period had come. I went to Mohamed, the driver, and asked for the keys to the car. I waited for the elevator, which took a few minutes to arrive, as we were on the sixth floor. Reaching the ground floor, I almost ran to the car. It was three minutes away and there were many people walking in the street, so I had to run between them to reach the car quickly. A little panicked, I took my bag from the car and returned quickly, waited for the elevator, went to the toilet and everything was okay. Now I just had to see how it would affect me. If the next two days passed without any problems, then my worst fear would really be assuaged.

I had a coffee, then we were all ready to go. It was two-thirty. I started the walk with Younes, and we walked through a very poor village, with houses built on a hill on our right hand side, painted in faded yellow and blue, and to our left green fields. There were children everywhere in the village and they were all so excited to see us. They waved to us and some came over to take photos with us.

Younes was a bit shocked and kept repeating, "They are barefoot; this is the poorest village we have walked through."

I wasn't as shocked: I have seen worse in Cairo. Once I was walking in old Cairo which had been the center of the city but currently it is a place that has artisans and craftsmen whom their talent isn't as appreciated as before; technology has affected them badly. This area has poor people at the moment and some of them live in a one room apartment without a ceiling. I was walking there to take photos because it still has remaining of historic buildings and many historic mosques. And suddenly a woman with a baby approached me and my friend and asked us to take her daughter. We were stunned; this woman couldn't afford to feed her daughter that she thought that well-off strangers will be kinder to her than their circumstances.

After walking for two hours, Younes realized that we were the last and lagging far behind, telling me that we should run to catch up.

I asked him, "Are you sure we are the last?" though I already knew the answer—I was buying time.

He told me, "Yes, Ahmed was running a while ago and he must be several kilometers ahead of us. Osama is ahead, Hamdy is ahead and Samy is ahead."

Though I said okay, I knew that I wouldn't be able to run because it was the first day of my period and typically I get short of breath in the first days.

I told him, "I will run with you after tomorrow."

My aim was just to say something, all the while thinking about whether to tell him that I wasn't feeling well. But my thinking process was too slow and wasn't leading anywhere.

We started running, but after less than 100 meters I couldn't breathe, so he told me, "It's okay, we can rest a bit."

After a minute, I told him that we could continue running, so we did and the same happened again repeatedly, until we reached the others.

We had 17 km remaining for the day, but it was already getting dark. The sunset was magnificent. There were yellow mountains on our right, very close to the road, and the Nile was on our left, dotted with palm trees. The sun was disappearing in the water. Sally, the new girl from the event management team, was in the support car and she came to walk with me. Younes was ahead of us with two of the Red Cross team and Ahmed and Osama were a long way ahead. When it became totally dark, Sally went back to the car and I walked with two members of the Red Cross team.

My energy was rapidly draining and I just wanted to sleep. There was a breeze of fresh air, so I closed my eyes for a while and kept walking, asking my companions to tell me if I was going to hit something on the road. They told me that I would get dizzy and I kept walking with my eyes closed for another few moments until I did get dizzy and I opened my eyes. The weather was glorious, but I was starting to feel a bit cold. I went to the car to put my jacket on. When we had finished 10 km of the 17 km that remained, we decided to call it a day. It was already seven pm and we still had a long ride to the hotel. Osama rode in the other car, while Ahmed, Younes, and I rode in our car. I was in the front, with Ahmed behind me and Younes behind Mohamed.

Fifteen minutes later, Osama sent us a message on our WhatsApp group. An article had been written on the challenge. We had seen it when we were in the youth center and we liked it. All our names had been written and we were mentioned in the post on Instagram. The article had been written because of Younes's connections and it featured in one of the most widely read magazines by people in our social circles in Cairo. It was really nice but then when we were there in the car, Osama sent another message asking if any one of us was supposed to be leading the others, because he had thought that we were collectively participating, without a leader. The article had said that Younes was leading the group. I looked at Younes and showed him Osama's message.

He told me, "I will talk with him when we arrive."

After a few moments of silence, Younes continued, "But I don't know why this would bother anyone, because it's the truth."

I looked at him and said, "I know that it is your idea, but it is led by both you and Ahmed."

I remembered then Ahmed's words that actions show the real ethics. But I also remembered that I had thought that this was Ahmed's idea as well. Younes had always been calm, but what happened next I didn't expect at all. Younes started stating everything he had done to make the challenge happen. So I told him that Ahmed had also done some things. Younes didn't listen, or at least didn't appear to listen and he repeated again that he had planned the route, he had secured most of the sponsors and he was the one who had given the presentation to our main sponsor. He kept stressing "I am the one who did this" in response to each sentence I uttered, before finally telling me "I don't like saying 'I, I, I' . . . but I'm telling you what happened."

I didn't like seeing him like this. He was jumpy and tense. Though I didn't take his words lightly, his nerves seemed frayed and he almost appeared like an overwrought child, looking for comfort. It was clear that he was trying to contain himself, but what he was holding inside seemed too much for him to handle anymore.

And Ahmed was silent. He had told me before, "Why put effort into a war that someone else is fighting?" But I wasn't fighting for him; I wanted to know the truth.

I told Younes that I had seen Ahmed managing operations during the last period. Younes frowned.

Ahmed told him, "Okay, so you did fifty percent of the effort and I did the other fifty."

Younes didn't like that.

Ahmed said, "Okay, you did seventy percent and I did thirty percent".

Younes didn't agree or disagree, but after a moment he said, "You keep saying that it is your idea and it is not."

"I stopped telling people that it was my idea after you mentioned this to me last time," Ahmed retorted.

"But I heard you today on the phone telling someone that it was your idea," Younes said.

"But he wasn't from the press or media," Ahmed said.

We were all quiet. I looked back out of the corner of my eye and found Younes sitting with his spine straight, his head leant back, and his hands resting on his legs. I didn't care to look at Ahmed. He had lost my respect but I was emotionally numb. I came to this adventure because I trusted Ahmed. I had mingled with Osama before the trip and had thought we were on good terms, but I didn't understand what was happening with him now. The person I had been the most worried about interacting with, beforehand, was the one who had been the nicest to me over the past five days. But still I had only known him for five days. I started to feel suspicious and that I couldn't make sound judgments, but I knew that I didn't like seeing Younes so down. I wanted to lighten the atmosphere a bit, so I put on some music, but it didn't change anything.

We arrived at an Italian restaurant, Pizza Roma.it, for dinner. They had prepared a long table for the team. Younes sat in the middle of the table, I chose to sit in front of him and Ahmed positioned himself at the end of the table, where he then kept going in and out of the restaurant all the time. We had placed our orders before arriving, so it was almost ready when we got there. I had ordered Lasagne Di Mare and had a small talk with the support team about the food and how good it was.

When we were finished, we went back to the hotel. I was feeling emotionally and physically tired, and was already not experiencing my best days. I was thinking that I should talk with Ahmed, but I didn't know what to say and I realized I truly didn't have the strength to do so.

Day 5
ASWAN
Edfu – Esna
35.4km – 7h 12m

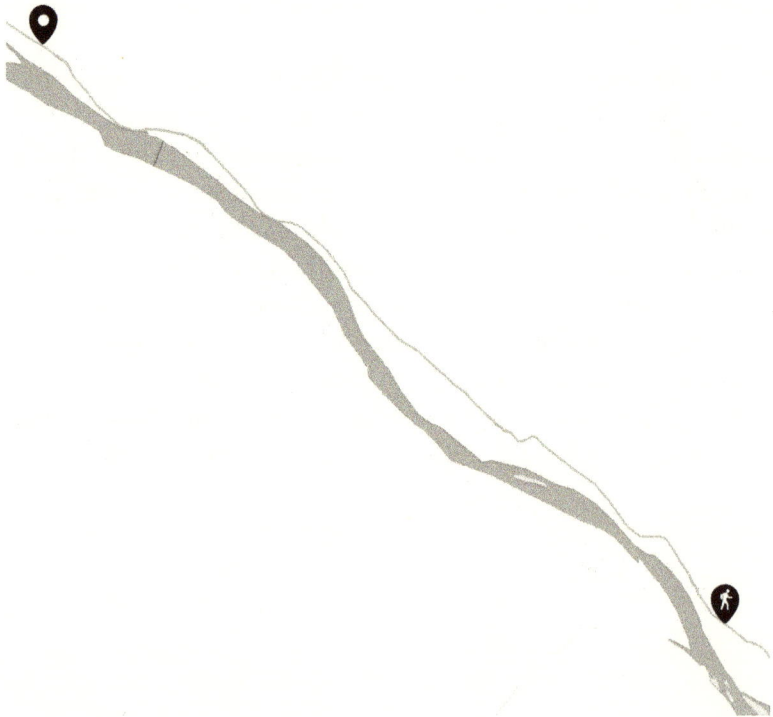

Day 6

THE PREVIOUS DAY, when it started, was a new day. This day wasn't. This day was the extension of the previous day. I woke up and found a message on the group from Ahmed that he had sent the day before when I was already asleep. It said that he would not join us that day. He would join the activities that we did at the youth centers but he would not be there for the sake of the challenge or the team anymore.

Osama didn't know what was happening so he had sent an exclamation mark and, in the morning, Younes said that we should all have a talk over breakfast. So we met over breakfast at six am. We were going to move at six-thirty that day, because Younes had said that we all needed to rest. The four of us were there on time and sat at the same table without any of the support team. Whenever any of them walked past us, they understood that something was going on, so they didn't interfere.

Ahmed said that he would not join the walk but that he was there with his bag so that no one would notice that there was a problem.

"What about when they see you sitting in the car? Won't they notice that you are not walking?" is what I wanted to say, but I didn't.

Younes started saying that he hadn't meant to upset anyone. He said that Ahmed and I were accusing him, so he was only defending himself. I told him that I hadn't intended to accuse him of anything; I was asking to clarify things. But Younes couldn't or didn't want to believe me. He said that he wanted us to stay a team and he didn't want Ahmed to leave. And he apologized for unintentionally hurting anyone. I also apologized to Younes in case my words the day before came across as accusations. I said that I was very thankful to them all because I was there thanks to input from each one of them. It was Younes's idea, Ahmed had told me about it, and Osama had helped me to train and his personality and spirit had encouraged me to join.

Ahmed started crying. I was touched and Osama asked me jokingly if I was going to cry as well. Younes was also touched and he stood up to hug Ahmed. As he stood up, I realized that he was tall. I hadn't thought of him as tall before. When he went to hug Ahmed, I found that they were almost the same height.

We all stood up to go to the cars. I was feeling light that day. Finally, I understood the reasons behind the coldness that had been in the air over the past five days. I felt that maybe now, when Younes had claimed his position in the team as the leader and things had been clarified, we would get more cohesive. I told them that we needed to do something, the four of us together, after the walk, but nobody really seemed to support me in that idea.

We reached the start line and, just like every day, Younes said *three, two, one* and we started walking. There was a canal on our right, with green fields running parallel to it and more fields on our left. Younes had his music on, Osama was walking at the head of the group, and after half an hour he told us to look at the canal. There was a Nile Monitor. It was our first time to see one and it is bigger than a lizard and smaller than a crocodile. But when it felt our presence, it disappeared into the water.

We continued walking under the shades of the trees. I was the last in the row and Ahmed was in front of me.

I walked ahead to be beside Younes and asked him, "So you appear to be calm, are you really calm on the inside as well?"

I knew that it was a weird question, but I wanted to ask it this way anyway. He looked at me with a smile and he said that it is very difficult to anger him. He told me that he hadn't had an easygoing life and had been pushed to the brink many times.

I had many thoughts running around my head. He had burst out last night after five days of taking all of what Ahmed had been doing. Ahmed hadn't only been behaving as if he was the team's project manager, he had also been bossy with the support team, even though he showed very little discipline sometimes. He was almost never on time. He took long rests, but got upset if something didn't work logistically or his food didn't come as he had "planned." The day before we had traveled to begin the walk, we had had a meeting with the event management company to share with them our nutrition plan—which we didn't have! And so he had made up one on the spot.

I was wondering whether Younes was waiting for the right time to claim his right as the leader. Or whether he felt he wouldn't have many opportunities to do so as long as things were going the way they were going. We were already facing daily physical stress and, on top of this, emotional stress made it difficult to react at the right time with the right force. Our only choices were to reveal what was on our minds impulsively or to wait until we had absorbed the situation, made sense of it and then and only then, make a move. I guessed that Younes had been registering everything to make a move and that when he had the chance, he took it; His feelings had burst out of him in the car, when he stated everything he had done to make the challenge happen and clearly stated that he was the leader. Frankly, I didn't understand then what the importance was of who the leader was, but I later learned that it makes a difference when it comes to building the Curriculum Vitae of an athlete, which then helps secure sponsors for future challenges. But I also understand that seeing someone steal your idea and effort purely for fame is galling, and should be resisted.

"But I don't like to upset anyone" he continued.

"You are sensitive," I said, and he affirmed that he was.

I wondered, can one's weakness also be a strength? Is being sensitive a weakness or a strength? Is being nice a weakness or a strength? Personally, I admire people who show their vulnerability as well as their more obvious strengths. I see that when one has the ability to show their vulnerability, this is a strength in itself. And I know this because for years I wanted to show that I was a strong person, but hiding my weaknesses just turned me into a senseless robot. I found that hiding my weaknesses didn't make me any stronger; perhaps to others I appeared so, but fundamentally I simply lost myself to the idea of perfectionism.

"When I was a kid," Younes continued, "I had panic attacks. I was always scared that I would die and I did all the check-ups possible. Finally, I went to a psychiatrist until I learnt how to deal with my anxiety. But I still get afraid all the time. I am always taking care and looking around to make sure that things are safe."

I stared at him, but didn't notice it until I saw the look he was giving me in return.

This was news to me. I had never imagined that someone who could travel the world by bike would have such fears. I tried to contain my surprise, telling him, "It is very courageous of you to have such self-awareness and accept these challenges."

He smiled in return.

I told him a story. When I was a kid, I used to practice artistic gymnastics, and there was a move that I always did very well, called the back dive. One day I was on the beam and I just couldn't do it. Fear controlled my mind. The thing is, the more I thought about the move, the more scared I got. My coach tried everything with me, to help me. He tried to comfort me, tried to encourage me, but nothing worked. Then he decided to show me my worst fears. He made me stand on the beam and told me that he would count to three, and if I didn't do the move, he would throw me off the beam. He counted to three and finally threw me on the ground. The thing is, I wasn't afraid of falling; I was just afraid. And the more I thought of the technicalities of the move, the more afraid I felt. I spent more than a year afraid to do the move, until one day, I told him that I wanted to do it independently.

"Do you know, when I was young I had to have braces on for six years and after I was supposed to take them off, I had to wear them for another six months?" he said.

"I also wore braces, but for two years and I really suffered with them," I told him.

"These two teeth didn't grow," he told me, motioning to a part of his face. "So the whole jaw had to be pushed forward, so that I would have teeth in the front."

"It doesn't show at all," I said, looking at him. Maybe it was the first time to really see his face.

I had walked behind him for many hours, and knew his body structure perfectly now. But this was our first real talk. He is thin with strong, lean muscles. He has a thin face with a straight nose and small lips. His eyes are brown and almond shaped, and his looks are expressive. Sometimes his eyes shone from excitement and other times there was worry in them, but mostly they showed that he was constantly reflecting.

I thought about his teeth. This must have been real suffering, I thought. Does pain build a strong and sensible character? Does it make us submit to the idea that we don't own ourselves? We are living our lives, trying to be in control, because otherwise we feel lost. But when we get a simple cold, we realize that we cannot even control our bodies. He had to go through six years of pain and doctor's visits, and maybe not liking the way he looked, and maybe asking *why me?* in addition to the panic attacks. Did all that make him more thoughtful? Does he think of others because he understands that they might be going through hardship? I had so many questions about this person who I barely knew, but was certain that I wanted to know better.

He told me that a blogger had sent him a set of questions to answer. He read some to me and one of the questions was about what he thought of people generally. I asked him how he saw people. Younes has traveled almost half of the world on his bike. He has traversed Europe twice and visited many parts of Asia. He studied in Canada and has traveled around a lot. So he has met many people, of different nationalities.

He looked down, hesitant, and told me, "I think people are selfish."

I smiled, partly because I found it endearing that the thought that people are selfish made him sad. "I agree with you on that," I answered. "And frankly, it is not easy for people to be otherwise. It needs a philosophy in life. I recently saw some interviews with Jim Carrey, after people had said that he was going crazy. Have you seen them?"

He answered that he had not.

"He was at a fashion festival and it is unusual for him to be seen at such events. So the interviewer asked him, why he was there. He started talking about the meaning of things and about his belief that there was no Jim Carrey, in the sense of the well-known figure we think of when we hear the name. People made Jim Carrey. He believes there are no icons and no personalities, and that we are all simply a field of energy. I have seen different interviews with him and he is so inspiring. What I interpreted from his words is that we are all one. If only we all have this philosophy . . ."

We walked 21 km this morning, and though we all walked at almost the same pace, we were not walking together. We stopped for a photo when we reached a new city, Esna. Crossing the borders between governorates gave us the pleasure of a strong sense of achievement.

This particular day was hot. I poured water into my cap every now and then, but overall I felt good. The scenery was nice, with greenery or canals surrounding us to our right and left, and I had had a nice morning talk with Younes. Samy was walking with us on this day, but he was ahead as always. After 15 km walking Ahmed decided to run, saying that he felt better when he ran. Apparently his legs were hurting.

We reached our resting point. It was in front of a mosque and the Red Cross had come to join us. I went to use the toilet in the mosque and when I came out, I found Samy in the car with several of the people from the Red Cross around him. He had many blisters and they were applying mercurochrome to them. Then we went to a youth center in Esna. There were three groups, one a group of women and two groups of men. I went to talk with the women, while Younes went to talk with one of the male groups and Ahmed with the other. Younes was trying to sound local as he spoke with his group, but the truth is he sounded so foreign using the local dialect. This was funny but in a way that enabled him to get people engaged in his stories. Ahmed stepped in to talk with his group and started giving a speech right away.

I went to my group, which was made up of two distinct age groups: teenagers and mothers. Each sat on a different side in the group. The mothers were complaining that they did everything in the house and that they felt they didn't have their own lives, and they were afraid it was too late to make a change. And the teenagers were listening to their mothers, and they told me that they didn't want to turn out like them. I didn't have much time but I talked with the mothers, trying to help them think of small changes that they could make to give them some satisfaction and confidence. I thought it might help them to have some time for themselves, or to start walking every week as a way of taking exercise, to release negative energy and do something new.

I asked the teenagers what their aspirations were and together we thought about ways they could achieve their ambitions and about what would they do if something got in their way. I felt that these girls had a warrior spirit. Then Osama called me because the food had arrived and we needed to eat.

I went to the car and took my lunch box from the trunk and started eating. Samy was sleeping in the back seat of the car. He seemed very tired but it wasn't his feet that were ailing him at this point; he was shivering and dizzy. I was too hungry to pay proper attention to him and because he told me he was okay, I just concentrated on eating. Soon it was time for us to return to our walking point, and he went to the other car.

It was a nice ride, where we saw a beautiful old dam with an antique train on top of it. We were all excited and especially Osama; a friend had called and told him to look out for the dam, which is special in Esna. We had started to become appreciative of everything, no matter how small.

We reached our starting point, and Samy didn't join us. He didn't always take part in the walks because sometimes he had work to do. We were going to walk 15 km more on this day. My energy was draining and I don't know if anyone noticed that I was slower than usual, but Hamdy came and gave me molasses and told me to take a sip every now and then, and that it would give me some energy. I still felt a bit uncomfortable around him because of his attempts to flirt when we were at the restaurant, but I was trying hard not to let this show.

I was walking a bit behind the guys. Younes slowed down and asked me, "In the morning, when you told me that I apparently looked calm, were you talking about last night's incident?"

I answered "no" quickly, and added, "I learned that appearances are not necessarily reality, and I learned that every word has a meaning, so I said 'apparently' to show that I didn't really know, but was interested in finding out."

He nodded, but just then Hamdy came over to us and told us that Samy had been taken to hospital. He had come down with sun stroke and was being treated with medication. We learned that he would return to Cairo the following day.

Everything was changing so rapidly, and I was finding it so very tiring. I felt so sad. Samy had been my walking buddy, having walked with me at least half of the distance so far. I was getting really tired and it was getting dark. I asked Younes about the remaining distance we had to cover. He told me it was 4 km. According to my tracking device, we should have only 2 km left of the 35 km we were supposed to cover that day.

But we were getting used to this kind of discrepancy. Every day, we had virtually the same conversation: "What? 4 km? My device says only 2."

"Mine is the most accurate," Younes would always reply, seemingly impervious to the disappointment in our eyes.

After another forty minutes, he told us that we had 1 km left, then 100 m, and then we would start walking together, counting the steps until finally it was time to stop. And we would all smile or just lie on the ground.

One day, we asked him how many kilometers we had left, and he told us 2 km. Then after fifteen minutes we asked him again and he said 200 meters, but after a minute we asked him again and he told us 500 meters. Osama and I started yelling at him on this occasion, and he just smiled. I don't know if he meant this as a joke or if he simply made an innocent mistake. Younes did tell jokes from time to time, but they were always hidden ones.

That day, we had dinner at an Italian restaurant in the hotel. We all sat at a big table, had a nice dinner, and then went to our rooms. Osama asked Mohsen to come to his room. That day, Osama and Ahmed were excited because we were getting the BCAA, which is a supplement that hastens recovery. I had read a bit about it and found that it had side effects, so I had decided I wouldn't take it. And Younes doesn't like to take anything that interferes with his body. He likes it to recover on its own, so he is essentially against medications and supplements.

I went to my room, had a shower, and took a painkiller because I didn't have the energy to suffer through two hours of pain before taking medication, and because I thought it might regulate the flow. Then I slept immediately.

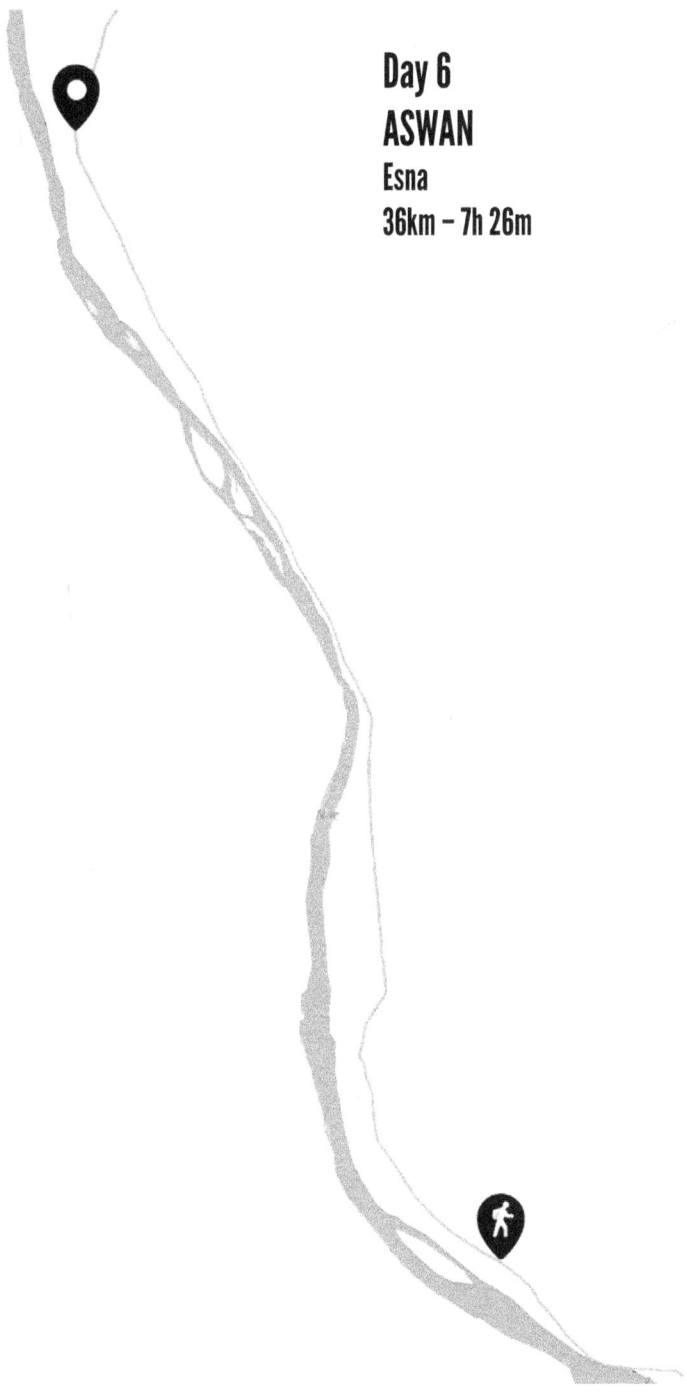

Day 6
ASWAN
Esna
36km – 7h 26m

Day 7

ANOTHER MORNING BROUGHT surprises and other unforeseen changes. I was barely able to wake up, but somehow managed to get out of bed at five-thirty am. I quickly dressed into my habitual outfit and put my jacket on, prepared my bag, and started my ten minute morning walk to the restaurant. On my way to the restaurant I met Hamdy, and he accompanied me on my regular route but in the middle of this he told me that there was another shortcut. I didn't believe him because it just didn't make sense. We arrived at the restaurant, then Younes appeared. He had taken a different route and he confirmed that he had checked both routes on the map and there was indeed a shortcut.

We started our breakfast and I called Osama and Ahmed to check that they had woken up. Osama arrived and Ahmed answered the phone, telling me that he would meet us at the lobby. Osama was still just about to start eating, so Younes told me that Ahmed could come and have a quick bite. I called him again to tell him this, but his answer shocked me. He told me that his foot hurt so much that he couldn't walk to the restaurant. I hung up, looked at Younes and told him what I had just heard.

We all went to the lobby and found Mohsen with Ahmed, who said that he suspected a fracture of his big toe. It was so swollen that he couldn't stand on it. Hamdy said that he would take him to the hospital, but the doctors wouldn't arrive before nine so we would have to wait in any case. We were going to need to wait for two hours in the hotel.

Ahmed was in surprisingly high spirits; he started sending voice to text messages to everyone in the team. They started talking to Siri. Then they started playing a game of guessing the name of a movie without talking. All this time, I was sitting on a chair, leaning to my right or my left.

One of the support team told me, "I didn't know that you were an introvert."

"I am totally an introvert," I replied.

"I thought that was an insult," he said, laughing.

He might have been joking, but the truth is I am an introvert. I get my energy from inside, not usually from the people around me. But I was also drained. At these times, I find it is best to be surrounded by women, who I felt would understand that I needed chocolate and hugs.

Younes was sitting at the bar, with Hamdy, on his laptop. At first, I was curious to know what they were doing but I then dismissed the thought. I was glad to be able to rest, peacefully. The boys had left me to just be, without asking me to play with them. Then Younes came over with his coffee and sat on the empty chair next to mine. He put his cup of coffee on the table and I looked at it for a long time, before finally asking him if I could have a sip. I had two and felt a bit better.

He was still working on his laptop and by now I had deduced that he was calculating the distance and checking the routes to Cairo. I was interested to know how he was doing it but I only asked the question in my mind. Ahmed also wanted to learn how Younes was planning the route and calculating the distances, so he asked Younes to sit by his side with his computer, to see the routes. Younes went over to his side gladly. Hamdy came and told us that, as it was eight-thirty, a doctor would be waiting for us at the hospital at nine, so we could start moving. We went to the newly renovated, clean and shiny Luxor hospital, going straight upstairs to the manager's office. This manager turned out to be main doctor at the hospital, and also happened to be an orthopedic specialist.

Ahmed sat on the couch, took off his Crocs and socks, and the doctor examined his toe. The first thing he said was that one cannot get a fracture in the big toe. Fractures can apparently happen in the index toe and elsewhere, but not the big toe. Ahmed answered that it was his big toe that had been swollen the day before. The doctor replied that most probably this was inflammation from the effort expended, but nothing serious. He did offer to do a scan anyway, to make sure that everything was okay.

That was the first time that I realized that Ahmed was not as strong as I thought. Two days earlier, we had been taking a break and, because we had cooled down, I started to feel pain in my ankle and to be unable to move it properly. I had taken a look at it and found it swollen. I quietly asked Mohsen to come for a moment, showed him my ankle and he confirmed that it was swollen. I told him that I would apply anti-inflammatory gel on it and would keep an eye on it, and this was exactly what I did. I leaned a bit more on my left leg than usual and, during the lunch break, I applied the gel again and finished the day on foot.

I felt that I was being mean, but I couldn't control my thoughts and feelings. Maybe it was because I already had hard feelings towards him, or maybe I was frustrated because I felt that he needed so much attention. After his fight with Younes and Younes taking over the leadership role more completely, he seemed to need attention again. I wasn't sure.

We went to the cars and waited for Ahmed to have his scan. I found that my bag was all wet because water had been spilled on it, so I asked Mohamed to put it on the roof of the car in the sun. Hamdy and Ahmed came over, with the scan having revealed that everything was okay but that the doctor had said that it would be better for him to rest for a few days to make sure that he didn't develop a serious injury. We had to make a decision. Should we keep walking without him, or should we all stop for the day?

Ahmed told us that he didn't want to stop. Osama replied forcefully that if he didn't rest at least that day he might need to stop completely. Younes and I agreed. Younes said that we could all rest for the day. I backed him up and felt that I was lucky because I also needed that rest. Maybe we all did.

With the decision made, everyone agreed that we should rest that day and resume the next day. Younes suggested that we go and eat McDonald's and I strongly agreed. I don't usually eat fast food, but I badly needed a mood-enhancing meal. It was the first day since we had started the challenge that we hadn't eaten something grilled. And it was the first day that we didn't worry about starting early so that we could finish before sunset. And, I thought, this was the first day that we all mingled.

We arrived at McDonald's and I ordered a cheddar cheese melt combo. Everyone placed their order and we went to sit upstairs. We were all quiet, but I found a newspaper, grabbed it, and read out loud the title of the articles that I found interesting. Then I read the horoscopes. I asked everyone what their horoscope was and told them how their day was predicted to go.

I started with Sally, then Hamdy. Hamdy told me that his horoscope was the worst. I asked him "Scorpio?" He said no, Taurus. Privately, I thought that *was* the worst but I read his horoscope out. Then it was Younes's turn.

"What's your sign?" I asked.

"Guess," he answered.

I asked him, "What?"

He answered, "Scorpio," but I didn't get the joke then.

I read Osama's then; he is a Cancer. Then I read Ahmed's, and then the food arrived. Hamdy told me I didn't read mine out, and I told him that it was the same as Ahmed's. And this was one of the very few times that I didn't feel proud that to be a Libra.

We all ate, and my spirits were improving. I understood Younes's joke then—a bit late, I know, but blood was only just starting to flow in my head. Then we all started telling jokes. Osama had a big list of jokes, most of them long and silly but we laughed anyway. All this time, I found that Hamdy was staring at me. Without even looking at him, I could feel his eyes on me. I didn't understand what he could possibly be thinking of. Was he just day dreaming? I wasn't sure but I was uncomfortable.

I remembered that my bag was on top of the car, so I went to Mohamed and asked him about it. He told me that he had put it inside.

We started to make our way back to the hotel, walking past by Luxor Temple, situated just beside the Nile. It is this that makes even the most casual walk in Luxor splendid. The temple is a large, ancient Egyptian temple complex, constructed in approximately 1400 BCE. It is characterized by high open-flower papyrus columns. For thousands of years, the temple was buried beneath the streets and houses of Luxor and a mosque was even built over it. This mosque was carefully preserved when the temple was uncovered, and forms an integral part of the site today.

We talked about evolution. I don't remember how the topic was opened, but it might have been at the thought of our great ancestors.

They have been at the back of our minds as we discussed how human beings may look in one hundred years. There are body parts that, reportedly, we may not need in a century's time and toes are among them. Apparently, we don't use toes as much as we did in the past. Our ancestors used to hike more, and were often barefoot as well, while we are always wearing shoes. Another body part that we may be evolving not to need any more is wisdom teeth, which already many people have started not to get. It may also be a relief to know that the appendix is also apparently dispensable. We may not have it in the future, as it is not only useless nowadays but it also can get inflated and need to be removed. So one could argue that we would be better off without it from the beginning!

We arrived at the hotel and started thinking about what to do for the rest of the day. Ahmed was going to rest until lunch. Osama wanted to go to the gym and he told us that we should all go. I told him that I didn't want to and that I didn't want to tire my muscles. He told me that they wanted me to be like Nadia El Adany.

I hadn't seen this coming. Why would they want that? And who is "they"? Younes interjected, to say that everyone should do what they wanted. I felt relieved, as Osama had been causing me stress. Then Younes said he would go to the spa for a massage.

We all left and I slept for two hours. When I woke up I went to see Sally, whose room was just beside mine. We had been staying at the hotel for several days, but this was the first time that I had seen it in the sunlight. In Sally's room, we made some coffee. She told me that she wasn't sure why she had been hired. She had been interviewed in Cairo, then had received a call telling her that she was hired and that she needed to start working right away. She was told that she would start working in Aswan and would continue with us to Cairo. She wasn't told exactly what she would do.

She was, she told me, hesitant but as she was unemployed she decided to take the chance. She had arrived in Aswan and right up to that day, she told me that she hadn't been given anything to do. Hamdy wanted her to be with him all the time, but she just sat in the car. I was honest with her and told her that we were also astonished that they had hired someone new because there didn't seem to be much work there.

But Samy had left and Ramzy had plans to leave for a week, so we speculated that she might be needed then.

Sally is a bit taller than me. She has long, light brown hair and a light skin tone. She is curvy, and almost a bit chubby. We went for a walk and sat by the pool, which overlooked the Nile directly and offered a great view. Sally told me about her life in Alexandria, her home town, and her ex fiancé. She had been engaged to a man with whom she was deeply in love and very attached to. He had been extremely nice in the beginning, but over time he became so controlling. He kept telling her to cut out particular men from her life, and she did, then he would forbid her from going to particular places but she found out that he went to these same places himself.

Then she found out that he went out with other women. She wanted to break up with him, but he told her that they should talk and then didn't get back to her for weeks. As it is not uncommon within Egyptian culture for parents to get involved in these situations, his father called hers and asked that they forgive him, promising that he would be a better person from that time on. So she had hopes that he would change, but of course he didn't. He didn't even seem to care much, and then he broke up with her.

At first, she told me, she was so down. Then she decided that she would wear all the things he hadn't let her wear when they were engaged, and she decided to go to the places she had always wanted to go to and talk with people freely.

And guess what? He wanted to get back together with her.

And guess what she did? She rejected him.

Osama sent a message to say that he would go to the pool. I told him which pool we were at and he arrived with Mohsen. The water was intensely cold, so they sat with us for a while. I had my feet in the water to try to cure any inflammation. We talked, savouring the fresh breeze. The men decided to jump into the cold water and I took photos of them. Then Hamdy appeared and we all went for a walk with him. We went to the zoo, which is on the hotel island. Hamdy walked in the front with me all the way and Osama, Mohsen, and Sally followed us. I wasn't comfortable walking with him but whenever I slowed down to try to stay with the others, he kept walking quickly, and I didn't want to be rude.

We reached the zoo. After a few minutes the others caught up with us. Osama went to shake hands with the chimpanzee. I wanted to do the same but the chimpanzee wouldn't shake hands with me. Hamdy was watching me and started laughing. Then we found a swan, who was ill. Osama was angry that she was not taken better care of. We saw the zookeeper and Osama told him, with some force, to keep an eye on her. We then went back to our rooms.

I stayed in my room until lunchtime. It was supposed to be at five , then they said six , then finally they said seven-thirty. I was starving. We all met in the lobby and left for the Hilton. When we entered, it looked so extravagant. The hall was circular with columns on the side, and the ceiling was very high with drawings on it. Then between the columns there were different passages. We went into the passage in the middle, there were mirrors on the right and left, and then there was a huge bar in front with glass walls overlooking the Nile. Restaurants were on our right and left.

A reservation had been made for us, so they took us to a Thai restaurant with a set menu. I know that the event management company was trying to impress us, but we were in need of a substantial meal; we needed sufficient amounts of carbs and protein. At the beginning, it was only the four of us. Ahmed and Osama sat on one side of the table and Younes and I on the other. I left a chair empty between us. I always want to give people their personal space because I am sensitive to mine with most people; there are only a few that I feel really comfortable letting into my personal space. Younes had told me that he was an introvert so I assumed that he might prefer more personal space than most people.

Ahmed and Osama started teasing Younes about his walk, then his watch, and they were giggling like children, until the others joined us. The food started to arrive and it was small portions that I personally did not find tasty: we had soup, then chicken wings with dressing. The dessert, however—rice milk—was fantastic. Surprisingly, this was my first time to even try it, although we always have it at home. It was just delicious.

As usual at such gatherings, Osama started to make jokes. He told the Edfu jokes and laughed about how each person recounted a different story about how Edfu got its name. Meanwhile, we reminisced about the girls running after him. Osama, I decided, definitely had the strongest character of the four of us. He can make a scene in any place and he doesn't care about the looks he might receive.

I was feeling good that I was getting to know Younes and things were getting better between me and Osama, but it felt weird that the only person I thought I knew beforehand turned out to be someone that I didn't know at all. I was surprised to find myself on better terms with the two that I hadn't+ even heard about seventeen days earlier.

We finished dinner and returned to the hotel. We had all needed that rest day and now felt that we could wake up earlier than we had in the last days, to make up the kilometers that we hadn't covered that day. I started counting how many kilometers we needed to do per day now, and it seemed that we would have to walk over 45 km on some days. I started to feel scared that I might not be able to walk all the distance on some of the days. But I decided to leave that possibility to the future, and I slept.

Day 7 0 km

Day 8

AT FIVE-THIRTY AM Ahmed texted asking if we were going to meet at six. I told him that we were meant to meet then, at five-thirty, at the restaurant for breakfast. I was already there so I took a photo of my breakfast and sent it to him. He replied that, in that case, he would meet us directly in the lobby. Younes urged him to come anyway, for a quick bite, but Ahmed responded that he was not hungry, and that in any case he would eat sweet potatoes on the road. Apparently Ahmed had started to become more conscious of the fact that we needed to make use of every daylight hour to be able to complete our walk in the allotted time of twenty-four days, otherwise we would fail in our challenge.

At six-ten the four of us were in the lobby but the cars weren't ready. We called Hamdy and he told us that they would be there right away, but that the drivers weren't feeling well. As Younes had remarked on several occasions, the drivers were the most important part of the support team. We could always find a place to sleep or to eat when we needed to, but it is very hard to find drivers who would be ready to support us all day every day. And the ones we had were of a very high standard: supportive and professional. They weren't just driving normally, but had to keep their eyes on us all the time while we were on the road, had to drive at five kilometers per hour to keep pace with us, and they were responsible for car maintenance and even did errands for us sometimes after dropping us off. So their job wasn't easy.

That day, Mohamed wanted to leave. It turned out that the day before, after dropping us off late, he had had to go and do some errands and he was asked to wake up earlier than us to prepare the car and be ready when we were. It was impossible for him, and inhumane. Younes talked with him and with Hamdy. Hamdy decided to hire a third driver so we would have three cars for the team and the supporters. The drivers with the support team could alternate. Mohamed wanted to remain with us as our driver and supporter and he wasn't responsible for the errands anymore. By this point, we thought of his car as our car and we had become accustomed to his system and he to ours.

It was almost seven by the time we moved, and we reached our starting point at seven-thirty. There was a canal on our right and fields of crops on our left. After we heard the three, two, one that preceded our start, I put my earphones in and started listening to my German stories. We walked on the left side of the street, with Osama ahead and the rest of us following. Then Osama crossed to the right side under the shade. Because if we looked to our right it was due east, it was better in the early morning to have trees on our right and the road on our left. Younes followed, and then he looked at me as if to show that I should cross over to the right side as well, so I did and was walking by his side.

I asked him, "Do you speak German?"

He said that he didn't. He then asked, "Did you go to a German school?"

I said that I hadn't and started talking about my background. "I graduated from the Faculty of Languages, but then I worked in the field of business consultancy. I don't know if you went through something similar or if you had everything figured out when you were young, but when I was in high school I had no idea what I should study at college or what I wanted my career to be."

"I experienced the same thing," he replied. "I studied engineering for a year but then I realized that wasn't what I wanted, so I switched to economics."

"I spent my four years in college doing extracurricular activities and studied only in the last week so I would pass," I told him. "And when I graduated, I found work in a learning department at a very big corporation. I used to read books and present them to the management team. Then I worked in the training and consultancy field, and I've always volunteered in the entrepreneurship scene as well. I wanted to take my career in entrepreneurship forward, so I went to Germany to do my Masters, and that's how I learned a bit of German."

I realized I had told him a lot about myself. "And what do you do?" I then asked.

"I work in a family business. We serve as an agent for an engineering equipment company, selling and maintaining the equipment."

We walked in companionable silence for a while. "So what made you interested in the challenge?" he asked, after a few moments.

"I'd just resigned, and by chance Ahmed ended up telling me about it. I wanted to join immediately," I said. "You know, I've been telling people about how much I want to travel around Egypt for such a long time. It's very strange how things work out. If I'd tried, I couldn't have planned the sequence of events that way. Do you think that there is something greater than us that created everything?"

"I think the universe works in a miraculous way and we are only just starting to discover and explore its hidden depths," Younes answered.

"And do you believe that this power has consciousness? I mean, that it isn't chaotic?" I asked.

He answered immediately, "It's not chaotic."

As we walked, we passed the canal to our left, and the trees beside it gave us shade. We had been contemplating nature as we talked, with Younes periodically gesturing at the colors of the bougainvillea we passed, and whenever I noticed a unique bird, I pointed it out to him. I marveled at the shapes of the leaves and their different colors, and the movement of the water. At times, I felt that nature was a dance choreographer, and that if we paid attention to it we would learn how to dance.

"I want to be tough," Younes told me, as he came to my side.

I looked at him, a reluctant expression on my face for a second, then I told him, "You will reach an equilibrium."

He answered my look with a questioning one of his own.

"You will try to be tough, but after a while you will reach an equilibrium between your true self and being tough."

His pace slowed, as he reflected on my words.

I looked back at him, "But you know what? People aren't made of glass, I mean."

He interrupted, "I understand," but I continued anyway.

"I've been sensitive with people in the past, but then realized that they are tough to each other and to me as well. But we don't get broken." I took two steps forward, but then looked back at him. "And sincere people appreciate each other . . . no matter what."

He nodded.

It was getting warm and Osama asked if we would buy some caps to shade us from the sun. There were several options for caps we could have bought, but they were of poor quality so we hadn't done so. Younes told Osama that he had an extra one—a hiking hat with a back flap, just perfect for the walk. Younes had got sunburnt on his ears two days earlier but he hadn't taken this hat out. Instead, he continued to wear a regular cap like ours. Osama asked him why he hadn't worn his special cap, and he replied that he wanted all of us to be alike.

After walking 19 km, we reached a new milestone on foot: Luxor City. As always, the achievement felt amazing. We were going to walk for another 2 km before going to a youth center. The people we saw seemed noticeably different. Women were outside, either baking or working in the garden in front of their house. They still wore loose dark jilbab and long head scarves, but they didn't have to stay indoors as so many women had had to in Aswan.

We went by car to the youth center, which was in the middle of a village, Al Harajiyyah. It was 40 km away from where we had stopped walking, which wasn't pleasant for us. We were behind schedule because of the day we had spent resting, but we couldn't change the activity schedule we were committed to at the youth centers. Now on each day that we had an activity scheduled, we would have to travel there by car, which of course would be time consuming and would create a snowball effect, putting us ever further behind and compounding the problem.

To reach the village, we passed a bridge that ran over a canal and then there was a barrier beside the railway track that was closed, because a train was passing. We waited and I looked around, excitedly. Two boys were waiting beside us on their donkeys, as was a tuk-tuk with passengers in it and a huge truck. The boys looked at us with curiosity and white shining smiles. And I waited for the train to come. I was used to its sound by then, but there was something I found so dramatic about it, maybe because I associated it with departures.

The train passed and disappeared, but then immediately another one coming from the other direction appeared, before the barriers opened after a few minutes. It was chaotic, with everyone wanting to pass and the road partially closed, so that cars moved from one lane to the other, almost crashing into the cars that came from the other direction. After a couple of minutes, Mohamed figured out "the system" and we could follow it. It turned out there *was* a system behind this chaos!

We arrived in the village. It had very narrow streets, a gravel-covered, unpaved road and houses made mostly of red brick. After asking several people for directions, we reached the youth center. The managers were waiting for us at the door but we found that getting out of the car wasn't easy at all. After walking for four hours and then being in a car for an hour, with my knees bent, it was extremely difficult to actually get out of the car. I recognized the irony in this situation, as people were of course expecting to see strong athletes. It was hard for all of us, but Younes was the last to show it. Whether this was because he was good at concealing his pain or because he really didn't feel it, I don't know.

Mohsen was wearing shorts that seemed very short, given the culture, so I went to Younes and stood on my tiptoes to ask him in a whisper, "Are his shorts too short?"

He answered, "Maybe—I'm not sure." Then he asked, "Are mine?"

In Upper Egypt, it is not only women who are expected to dress conservatively, but also men. Any shorts need to be at least knee-length. I had noticed men and children staring curiously at Ahmed, who also wore shorts above his knees. Younes wore shorts that came to his knees, which was acceptable, and Osama was always in trousers or long shorts.

We went inside. There were a huge number of young people. We had been divided into two teams, with Osama and Younes together and Ahmed and I together. The crowd wasn't excited about seeing us, as it was hot and they had been playing in the sun for hours before we reached them. I talked to them briefly about the challenge and about how I had never imagined that I would be able walk this distance, to reach Luxor, and that the moral of the story was that if we really want to do something we can do it. Then Ahmed talked to them about population problems, and he was able to engage the crowd more than I did.

We left and went to see the other team. I found Younes taking selfies with the young people and everyone around him. When the girls saw me, some of them came over to me and told me that they had heard I had walked all the way to this point. They wanted to take a photo with me and I was so proud that my presence had this influence on the girls.

The day was moving so fast. We hadn't had lunch yet, and we had only walked 20 km in the morning. We went to Luxor for lunch then we headed to our starting point. By this point, it was already four-thirty and we knew that we would have to walk in the dark that day. Hamdy and Sally walked with us that afternoon but they were always in the front, walking quickly, and they looked tense. She was still always with Hamdy; when he appeared at the walks she was with him, when he went to work she was with him, and it seemed that there was still nothing much for her to do.

Ahmed was walking at the back a bit slowly. Since the fight and the injury, he had been quieter and either walked at the back or ran on his own. Whenever we were around, he was on his phone, texting. We found a message in our WhatsApp group from Ahmed, who was looking for Mohsen. Then when we next saw Ahmed and asked about his toe, he told us that it was his Achilles tendon that was really hurting him at that point. He told us that he was worried, because this is the strongest tendon in the human body and if it got injured, the whole body would be affected. I didn't know what the Achilles tendon was, but something didn't feel right to me. The previous day, he had had to rest because of his toe and now he said his toes are fine but his tendon was injured.

Was he planning to quit, I wondered. He had wanted to leave after the fight, or at least had pretended to. Were his injuries part of the psychological effect the fight had had on his body? If the Achilles tendon is the strongest in the body, would walking really cause it to be injured? Then I got scared, wondering that if walking could hurt your strongest tendon, what would it do to the rest of the body? I decided to dismiss the thought, and to wait and see what would happen next.

At eight-forty I asked Younes how many kilometers we had left. He told me two. The police were getting tired and bored, as we never usually stayed out that late. I didn't think that the police had to be with us all the time but in fact we were forbidden to walk without their presence, for security. In certain areas in Egypt the police secure foreigners traveling on particular roads, especially if they are traveling by bicycle or motorbike. We were sponsored by an international agency so we were considered to be under the jurisdiction and protection of the Exterior Ministry, so they insisted on securing us, even though it wasn't really needed. I gave them some fresh dates to say thank you, which, surprisingly, changed their spirit completely. They became patient and even encouraged us to finish the kilometers we had left for that day. I went over to Younes and told him that dates were miraculous; it must have been the sugar.

Finally, at 8:55 we finished our day's walk of 36 km. We knew that we were behind, but if we walked for longer we would end up sleeping too late and waking up too late. We feared getting caught in the snowball effect.

Over dinner in the hotel restaurant, we found the main sponsor who wanted to talk with us. We had to arrive in Cairo on the twenty-fourth day after the beginning of our trip, and they were worried because we were at least 40 km behind. They told us that they had calculated how many kilometers we had left and how many we would need to cover per day, and that we would need to walk 43 km per day to reach Cairo on time, without a rest day. Though we had planned our rest day on the sixteenth day, now we were learning we wouldn't be able to take it.

This was bad news, but not really news to us. It was the only way we could do it, by walking now for sixteen consecutive days. To do it, we would need to be committed and disciplined, and to move on time every morning. If someone was late, the sponsor told us, we would need to move on time and he could join us later.

After dinner, I told the guys that there was a shorter route to return to our rooms. Ahmed and Osama joined me, and Younes told us that he would follow shortly. The shortcut turned out to be longer than I thought, and the moment we reached our rooms I found Younes coming from the other route. He was smiling. I gave him a sideways look and told him, "I don't forgive you." We both laughed and each went to our room.

Day 8
LUXOR
Luxor
36km – 7h 24m

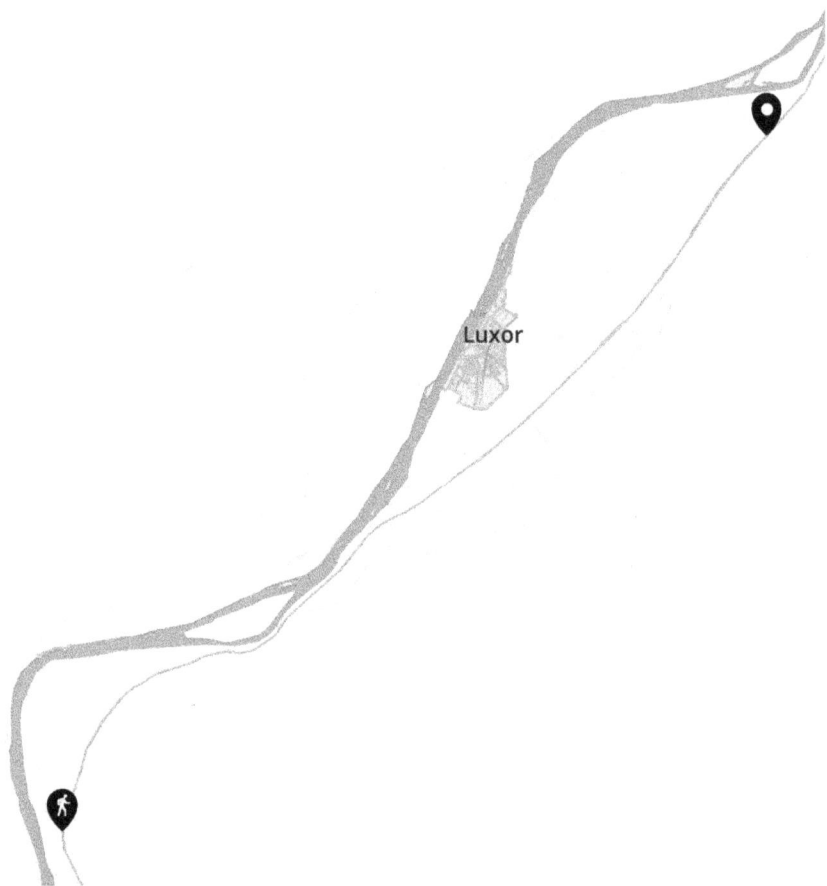

Luxor

Day 9

AFTER THE PREVIOUS day's meeting, we all felt an extra level of stress. We hadn't walked more than 40 km per day, and to walk 43 would mean we needed to be very disciplined and on time. We had talked, after Ahmed's injury, about following the plan that we had made at the beginning: starting early, having breaks every 10 km to rest and avoid injury, and to stretch.

We were all at breakfast on time. Over breakfast, Osama said that he thought that we should start waking up early and begin the walk with the sunrise. I looked at him in astonishment, yet with happiness. I had a very wide smile that I knew I should hide, but I couldn't.

I told him, "Finally this is coming from you."

He looked at me. "You are always late."

I was speechless and stared at him in disbelief.

Ahmed looked at him. "What are you talking about? She is the one who wakes us up every day."

We were all ready at six-thirty and we reached our starting point at seven. The walk started with us passing yet another governorate border. After a few kilometers, we found ourselves in the governorate of Qena. All I could think to myself was, wow. We had walked through Egypt's longest governorates, and I was still standing!

I started to ask myself if it was possible that I would walk it all. In the beginning, I had had more doubts than confidence, but now I saw myself as having a fifty-fifty chance. The pain I had at night was decreasing, and I was becoming fitter every day. Before the trip, we had measured our body mass index and I had been told that I needed to lose eight kg of fat and gain four kg of muscle. I knew that I had lost a few kilograms and that the muscles I needed for the walk had been strengthened. But I still didn't know how much my body could endure.

We took a photo under the "Welcome to Qena" sign. Then I started walking with Younes and asked him about Ahmed's injury. I was still worried that I might get the same injury. He told me, "If you knew what endurance sports do to our bodies, you would really be scared." I got more worried, and I didn't want this feeling to increase, so I told him not to tell me any more. Then I started wondering aloud how he had chosen the team. Younes told me about meeting Ahmed at the company activity session for the first time, and he had thought that Ahmed was an expert in planning sporting events and a good athlete. So then, when Younes had the idea of crossing Egypt on foot, he had contacted Ahmed, and been heartened by the way Ahmed was excited about the idea immediately.

Ahmed, meanwhile, already knew Osama and thought that he would be a good third companion. When Younes met Osama, he agreed that he would be a good fit, and then they had a team. I wanted to ask him how he felt when Ahmed told him about me joining, but I didn't. I was still afraid.

I found our walk that day so exciting. There was a canal on our left, and to the right another very small canal, with villages behind it. Both sides were connected by a series of bridges. Whenever we passed a village, children would cheer, call out to us in English, "Hiiii! Hiiii! Helllooooo!" and smile widely from the other side of the canal. And we would reply back. They would ask for pictures and the guys took selfies with them. For the kids we had the exoticism of foreigners; they didn't realize that we were Egyptians like them. Of course, they weren't used to seeing three men and a woman walking along the main road wearing sportswear, so it is little wonder that they were confused!

As we walked between the villages, I had small, deep talks with Younes. "You know, I feel lost. I always feel that I am floating. I do things to feel grounded, but then I get suffocated so I break free," I told him.

"What are you looking for?" he asked.

"I'm searching for stability," I answered, and we looked at each other and laughed.

"You are in the wrong place," he said, smiling.

"Yes, I'm aware of that!" I replied.

Then after a few seconds I continued, "This happens when we have contradictions in our personalities."

It was true, but crazy, that even though I was searching for stability, I had chosen to do the most spontaneous thing—leaving everything behind and attempting to walk the length of a country. Before actually embarking on the trip myself, I had thought that it was a crazy plan and I had talked about it as a joke. "There are three guys walking from Aswan to Cairo, haha!"

"But you know what?" I told him, "The most important things for me are values."

He nodded.

"There is an exercise that I do every few years, which reveals to me what is most important to me. I use it to make sure that everything I do is aligned with my values, otherwise my life doesn't make sense to me in the same way. It is like my compass. But still sometimes I get annoyed at myself for always doing different things, and then I feel a real eagerness to start something new."

"It's okay to be experiencing life," Younes said. "Our priorities change, and that changes our plans as well."

We had walked 10 km, and I decided that I would be responsible for making sure we had our breaks. There was a huge tree offering a lot of shade, so I took off my shoes and was preparing to stretch under it. Younes came over and said that it was a nice spot, and then he looked at me and told me that he wanted to pee. I looked at him in surprise and walked away to give him privacy. Then Ahmed came over and also wanted to pee. I started to walk away, and told them jokingly, "For me it's the perfect spot for relaxing and for you, for peeing!"

Then I finally got my chance to go stretch. I started doing some lunges, but then Hamdy walked past and asked me with a smirk, "Do you need help?"

I gave him a look that said "go away," and told him, "No, thanks!"

He replied with a smile, "I was going to tell Mohsen to help you."

I felt very frustrated. This attention I was getting from Hamdy was unwanted and made me very uncomfortable. I didn't know if I should tell someone about it, but I also didn't know who I could tell.

After a half hour break, we continued our walk and a group of PE students from the South of Valley University came to join us. But this time, there were no girls so I walked alone at the front. Younes walked just behind me, and Osama and Ahmed were with the guys at the back.

The scenery changed a bit, with the canal on the right disappearing and villages built directly beside the road consisting of small houses with very narrow roads. The roads were sandy and the houses were made of red brick or painted in light colors. I kept greeting people as I walked past, "As salamu alaykum." This is a greeting in Arabic and is the most common among Muslims or in Egypt in general. It is a religious salutation which means "peace be upon you."

"Wa alykum as salam," they would respond which is the typical response and means "and peace be up on you." Then they would add, "Come and have a tea," and I would answer, "Thank you." Later Osama joined me and asked me if anyone got offended from my response. I didn't get what he was referring to. It turned out the when I reply with a *thank you* for an invitation it means that I am rejecting the invitation and Osama told me that there was a better response: "May grace be multiplied to you."

Whenever I encountered children, I would try to stop and talk to them for few moments. I found five girls walking in the same direction I was, some of whom wore headscarves and jilbab and others who showed their hair and wore trousers and t-shirts. I asked them if they would like to walk with me and they said they would. They told me that they were on their winter vacation and they were taking private lessons in classical Arabic to strengthen their language. They told me that they were good at all their other subjects but that classical Arabic grammar was hard. I agreed with them, as classical Arabic grammar wasn't and still isn't easy for me. The spoken language in Egypt is Egyptian Colloquial Arabic which is the language of everyday life and the most widespread regional dialect of Arabic. It is based on classical Arabic but there are structural differences and some variations in the vocabulary used.

We reached the home of three of the girls, so they said goodbye and left. The other two girls continued their walk with me. I asked them about what other activities they did during their vacation, and they told me that they played in front of their houses with their neighbors. I told them about our walking challenge and about how important sport is for health and self-confidence. Then they reached their houses, we said our goodbyes and I continued walking.

So far we had walked 22 km in five and a half hours and we decided that we would take a break when we got to the start of the 25th. The event management company had our food ready, and after walking for another forty minutes we stopped. We got into the cars and made our way to the nearest village, to find a place to eat. We arrived at Qus in just ten minutes and we asked where we could find a cafeteria. It turned out to be a huge tent made of khayamya cloth, a few minutes' drive away. We went inside and found that it was full of men smoking shisha, and that the TV was showing belly dancing. We found space to sit together.

We were sitting beside each other on wooden seats around a wooden table. We took off our shoes, and Mohsen passed by with ice bags. Giving me one, he told me to put it under my feet to cool them down. Ahmed and Osama did the same and even Younes, for the first time, took off his shoes while we were resting. He sat straight-backed on the seat, as always, and only took off his shoes for a short while. I wanted to lie down somewhere, but it wasn't appropriate for a woman to lie down in such a place. There are many cafes in Egypt which are considered "men only" cafes. They sit comfortably, smoking shisha, playing backgammon, cursing and not watching their words, and watching belly dancing on TV. Women are not forbidden to enter but the atmosphere is not welcoming. When I was there no one showed me any unkindness but I wasn't comfortable and was on my guard.

Ahmed found a hidden area and asked Mohsen to go with him for a recovery massage session, and Osama asked the waiters to change the channel. The belly dancing was so provoking; Belly dance is a traditional dance in the Arab world but like most dance types, the moves can be sensual or sexualized. On this channel the moves were too alluring to be displayed in a café at noon so they changed it to another music channel, but still played very loud and disturbing music.

Then Osama decided to lie down right in front of us. Younes was just beside me, and changed to another seat. Even though I wanted to do the same, I was too numb to move or think.

This was the first day I realized that Osama was really injured. He had blisters on both of his feet and they were hurting him with every step he took. He had known that he would get blisters before we started, and he had taken precautions, applying some natural remedies to toughen his feet, but he still got them. Ahmed also had blisters, but they were few and not very serious. Younes didn't have any and nor did

I. I started to feel even more worried about getting injured—if not in my Achilles' tendon, then maybe I would get blisters.

The food had arrived, and it was the usual: rice, grilled chicken, and vegetables. My appetite was decreasing so I ate a few spoonfuls of rice, a few spoonfuls of vegetables, and quarter of a chicken.

After eating, we drank tea and I had French coffee. Younes always drank tea on our trip because, he said, "You can't go wrong with tea." With coffee, we knew that we always risked the quality of beans. We rested a bit more, and then we left to return to our starting point. There were trees on our right and left, and they were curved inwards touching as if they were an arch for us to walk beneath. I was charmed by it.

After 5 km, I could feel that I was already getting tired. We had planned to walk 45 km that day! Though it was ambitious, it had seemed possible when we decided to do it. So far, we had walked 30 km and we had 15 left before the day ended. I was waiting for us to cover another 5 km so that we could have our 10 km break. Osama was ahead of us, Younes and I were walking at the same pace, and Ahmed was a bit behind us. After another 5 km, Osama was still striding out in the front, Younes didn't want us to stop, and it was getting dark. However, I decided to stop for five minutes anyhow and Younes continued walking.

I was resting in the car when Ahmed reached me and asked if everything was okay. I told him I was just resting. He went to pee in the bushes and when he returned, we started walking together. Suddenly, he decided to run so I was all alone behind the others, and it was getting darker every moment. I put on my earphones, deciding to do my best to enjoy the walk, but I was tense. After half an hour, I found Younes waiting for me.

I asked him, "Why are you waiting for me? I'm fine." And we continued walking.

The sun had totally set and we only had the street lights to guide us. Or so we thought. Suddenly, even these lights went off because of an electricity cut and we found ourselves in complete darkness. I stayed with Younes, watching every step as the street was not even, and there were rocks and sand on the pavement. We were aware that there was a canal on our right, that we could fall into at any time. We were also a bit worried about the guys, but then discovered that Osama wasn't so far from us and that Ahmed must have finished the final kilometers, running.

The Red Cross rescuers came to walk with us. They let us walk on the inside and they walked outside by the street. They wore suits with light reflectors, so they could be seen by the cars driving along. I kept asking them to come closer in, as I was worried that a fast-moving car wouldn't see them. After over an hour of walking carefully and feeling stressed in the dark, the electricity returned and we reached our destination point. We had walked 45 km, despite the darkness. And we jumped into the cars quickly to go for food.

We went to an Indian restaurant, but Osama didn't come with us. He decided that he would eat in the hotel to be able to sleep early. While waiting for our food, Hamdy started asking about some of the details of our route. Ahmed wanted to reply, but then obviously realized that he didn't know the answer. Younes gave him a side look—he had known that Ahmed wouldn't know the details, but he still made him prove it. Then Ahmed and Hamdy both looked at Younes, so he told them the distance left and the route we were going to take.

We were ready to leave and I noticed that Sally hadn't said a word over dinner. I asked her if she was okay and at first she said she was. Then I asked her again, and she replied that she had a headache. I told her that I had painkillers if she needed them, but she assured me that she was okay. We had to leave the restaurant, leaving her and Hamdy behind, but I felt that something else had been going on. I was worried, especially because she looked as though she had been crying.

We reached the hotel at 9:45 and took the shuttle bus to our rooms. I stepped off the bus, and walked slowly, lost in thought. Since we were in the car, I wasn't feeling good about myself. I waited for Younes, until I could see that he was just behind me.

I turned my head towards him and told him, in a low voice, "Thank you."

He blushed and asked, "For what?"

I replied reluctantly "For waiting for me. I would have been scared if the electricity had gone off and I was alone."

"I couldn't have left you alone," he replied.

Qena

Day 9
QENA
Qaft
45km – 9h 1m

Part 2

By this point, we had walked almost one third of the total distance, we had crossed two governorates and entered the third, the team had settled into a rhythm and the support team had got used to a certain system, though one member had been injured and left us. Now in this part of the story, we will cross four governorates, stay at four hotels, and meet four different teams from the Red Cross, along with four police security teams and youth within each of these governorates. Some things will change in this part of the challenge—and, among them, the team that started its journey on eight feet will end it on four.

Part 2
QENA – SOHAG – ASSIUT

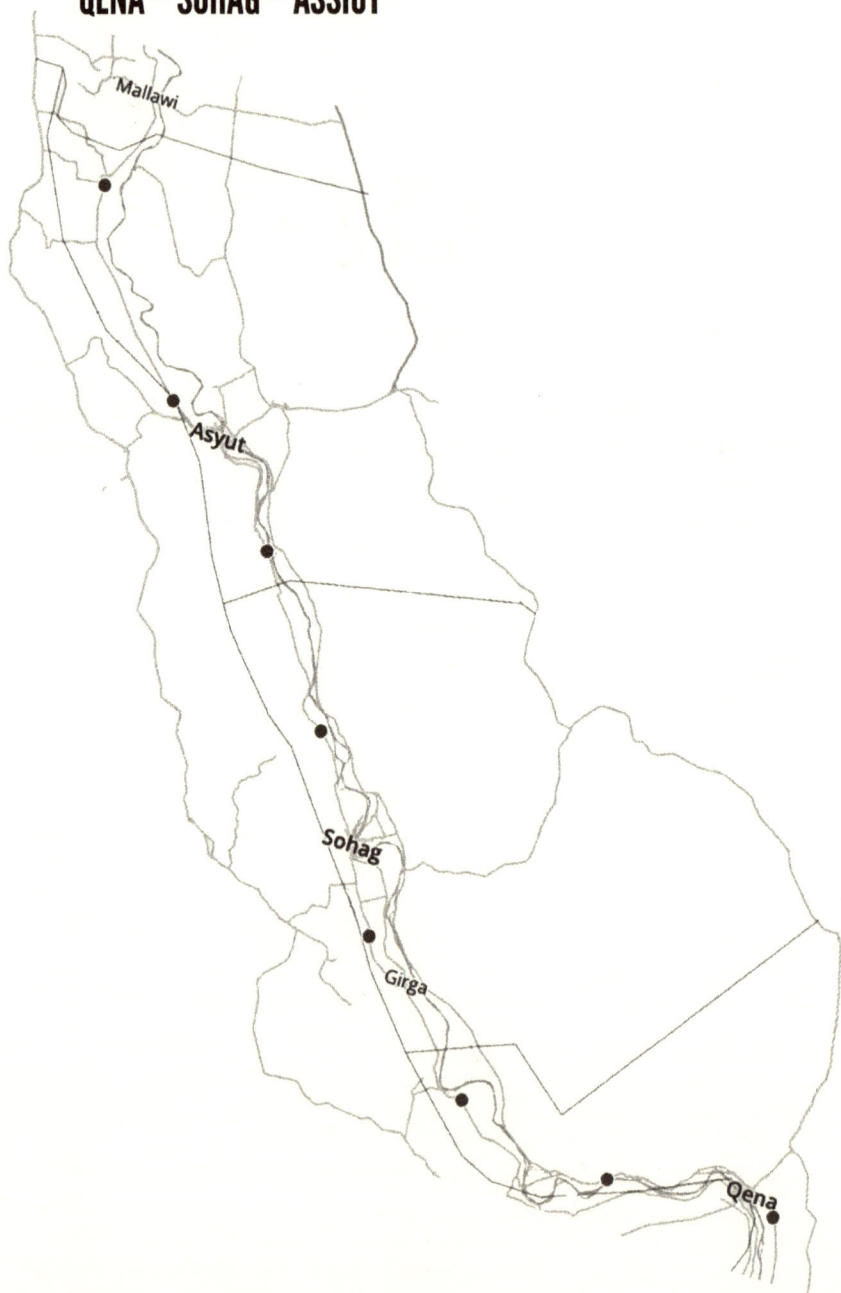

Mallawi

Asyut

Sohag

Girga

Qena

Day 10

AS THIS DAY started, I was feeling betrayed. I had become used to having an early snack with the others, but the previous day Younes had said that he would meet us in the lobby at five-thirty am and would take a breakfast box and Osama and Ahmed agreed to do the same. I couldn't do the same, as I need my morning French coffee to start functioning, and I had got used to having cereal as a snack. I left my room a little after five and started my walk to the restaurant in the dark, knowing that I would be alone. Being alone doesn't usually irritate me, and many times I walk alone on the road, but I hate eating alone. I arrived in the restaurant at five-ten, had my snack, and headed to the lobby seven minutes late. Younes was there, and Ahmed and Osama arrived shortly after.

It was still dark outside, and cold, and we were waiting inside for Mohamed to bring the car but he was late.

Younes was checking his phone and suddenly told Ahmed, "Sally has left the group!"

We had a WhatsApp group for the whole team and another for the four of us.

Ahmed quickly replied, "We shouldn't jump to conclusions—maybe she left by mistake, or maybe she had to travel and will come back. So let's wait till tomorrow and see what will happen."

Younes looked at Ahmed with disapproval, but said nothing. I guess Younes didn't like being passive and just waiting to see what would happen; he preferred being proactive and understanding what was going on. It seemed that my worries had been well-founded. I made a mental note to call and check on her when the sun had risen.

We drove for an hour and a half, until we reached our starting point. Younes told us on the way that after the next 22 km, we would have walked 300 km in total. This was a milestone that we wanted to celebrate—having covered almost one third of the whole distance, we felt sure that any of us could complete the full distance. It wasn't farfetched ambition anymore. The four of us were excited and buoyed by this realization, and we started our walk together that day.

The fields were on our right and small canal running beside us on our left. There were very tall trees by the canal full of birds sleeping on their branches. Our daily routine had become one where we started before the birds woke up and finished after they slept—or at least that's what it seemed like. We stopped to take photos of the birds on the trees and continued our walk. That day, a new team from the Red Cross was joining us and planning to stay with us until we had crossed the governorate of Qena. A few members of the support team were also going to be walking with us during the first half of the day. One of them was from the city of Qena. We called him Mimo, and he was so excited to show us around. Mimo was of medium height, with a shaven head and always dressed in jeans. He had -bowlegs, and we later learned that he had had many surgeries, yet he was fast and always active.

After walking for 6 km, we reached a huge mosque. Mimo told us that it was called Sidi Abd Er-Rahim El Qenawy. It was preceded by a huge garden, with a fountain in the center. Younes read the date of establishment and we were all amazed that it could be considered a monument. Having been built in 1127 BC, it was almost nine hundred years old. The mosque was earth colored and built in the Ayyubid architectural style, with many arches at its entrance, decorated with ornaments and Arabic calligraphy.

We stayed there for fifteen minutes, before realizing that we had to move. Leaving, we found ourselves heading towards the city. The streets were busy with cars and were much wider than any we had encountered so far. We saw two lanes for each direction and, overarching, a pedestrian bridge with escalators. The city's main street could well be considered the most modern we had encountered so far. As we walked, we found ourselves looking around to avoid the cars. Tall buildings flanked us to our right and there was a canal on our left. The buildings we passed housed many shops and other facilities, including pharmacies, banks, restaurants, and shops for tires and car spare parts.

After passing the center of the city we were already thinking about food, although it was still too early for lunch. Mimo recommended a newly opened Italian restaurant to us, which he spoke of with great excitement. Younes and I were ready to go there but Hamdy said that he had other plans for our lunch, namely taking us to a more "authentic" place, so we got more excited about Hamdy's choice.

I asked Mimo about life in Qena, and especially the situation for women, which interested me greatly.

"I've noticed that the further north we go, the more women are in the streets and public areas," I told him.

"There are villages in Qena where women don't appear at all, except in front of their relatives or people whom they consider to be relatives," he replied. "Once I went to a village and I found there were no women. It was as though they were all hiding, and it would have been considered a scandal if I had seen one without her being fully covered from head to toe. But I had work there, so I went frequently. Eventually, I was considered a member of the extended family, and it was okay for women to appear in front of me—and others like me— without their veils, even to the extent that they didn't hide when they were breastfeeding."

After another 4 km, we stopped to rest and, as always, I wanted to pee. There was a canal on our left and Qena's traffic station on our right. I certainly wasn't going to pee by the canal, so Mimo told me to go with him and that he would take me to the traffic station. I went with him and, while entering, the guards at the door stopped us, asking where we were heading. He told them that I just needed to use the bathroom. They searched my bag as a security check and let us in. When I came out, I found the guys sitting comfortably in our car so I went to the support car, took off my shoes, and lay down for a while.

I saw Younes looking around, then heard him asking about me, so I gestured to show where I was. He told me we needed to get ready to resume our walk in five minutes, so I started to put on my shoes and went to our car to take my bag, and just before we left Osama decided to go to the toilet. He also went into the traffic station and got checked, as I had. After ten minutes of waiting, we decided that we needed to start again and then Osama came out and joined us.

"I shouldn't have to tell everyone at the end of each break to get ready," Younes told me and I agreed. I knew that he was frustrated about Osama's timekeeping, but I guess he also wanted me to be more responsible.

After we had walked for another 10 km and spent a total of four hours walking that day, we stopped to take our lunch break, heading to the restaurant that Hamdy had recommended. We took the cars and went back to the city of Qena. We were impressed with the city's architecture, its design, and its cleanliness. To be honest, we hadn't expected cities in Upper Egypt to be this artistic; it was illustrative of just how much culture there had been there. Mohamed parked and we went into the restaurant, Abdo Kebab. Mimo told us that they had recently redecorated the place, so its originality had disappeared. The wall was covered with pictures of the place from decades ago and this was the only way its beauty had been preserved: in photos.

The four of us sat together on one table, with the support team on other tables, as the food started coming. We feasted on rice, vegetables, and grilled meat—kebab and kofta—the best we had had so far, and we had eaten grilled meat and chicken everywhere. We shared zucchini, peas, potatoes, and okra, all cooked with tomato sauce in the oven. We enjoyed every bite and wanted to wash everything down with a hot drink afterwards but they only served soft drinks, so we left, hoping to find a coffee shop in the street.

As we left Abdo Kebab, we passed a shop where the men expressed curiosity about what we were doing. I told them about the walking challenge. With astonishment, they asked us, "But why are you doing this walk?" I told them about the population growth issues we were trying to promote, and how we wanted to raise awareness as we passed through each city and met young people in their centers. They then started to have something to relate to. One of the guys told me, he was at a wedding last week and asked me to guess how old the bride was. I guessed fifteen, but she turned out to be thirteen.

My face must have registered shock and disbelief, and I asked them how that could happen and what she could possibly know about marriage. They asked me how old I thought the groom was. Then they answered: fifteen. I was horrorstruck. A groom of fifteen and a bride of thirteen . . . oh my God. They told me that nothing would ever change and that our efforts were in vain. I left with an acute feeling of disappointment, but also with something to think about. Why were communities doing this?

We returned to our starting point to continue our walk. After fifteen minutes we found Hamdy approaching in one of the support cars surprising us with cups of coffee. I was very thankful then that I could resume my day fully powered.

One of the people from the Red Cross walked with me for the first part of the afternoon. He was a philosophy teacher in a high school and also a farmer. We walked past fields of trees and he told me that they were mango fields. It was nice to see different trees, for a change, as we had been walking mostly by sugarcane or banana fields. He told me more about the city of Qena, which reportedly has the highest rate of crime in all Egypt. But people there often don't consider what they do to be crimes, but rather as taking their rights. So there are families that consider that they have "rights" that need to be taken from other families and this right does not actually consist of money or land but actually represents souls. So there are issues of revenge that date back decades and never end. One of the villages that is most infamous and feared in this regard is called Samta, and we were due to reach it shortly.

Younes was walking with one of the Red Cross members and I was just behind them when I found him pointing back at me and told the guy that I was the expert in that matter. They were talking about entrepreneurship and the guy had applied for a startup program but he wasn't accepted. He thought that it was all a hoax and they only accept relatives and friends because he believed that his invention was genius. I told him that each entrepreneurship supporting entity has its own criteria and he needs to know it by researching the entity before applying: to know whether his project fits the criteria or not and to customize his presentation to address their needs. Entrepreneurship is still new in Upper Egypt and it seems that youth with ideas don't have sufficient information on how the ecosystem works.

It was almost 4 pm when we reached Samta. Younes was in the front but just few meters ahead of the rest of us, and Osama was behind me, but also less than a hundred meters away, with Ahmed at the very back. Everyone was tense except me. I saw a young boy holding a weapon on a horse, in the village, 50 meters away. Then there were kids, curious, looking at us and waving hello and goodbye, so I waved back. Then suddenly I found almost ten kids running in the fields alongside us, running in the same direction we were walking in, to come and meet us. There was a canal separating us, but we saw several bridges that allowed people to cross the canal.

When the children reached me, they had wide smiles on their faces and they started asking what we were doing there. Everyone from the support team and the Red Cross was worried that interacting with these children would cause us problems, and they kept telling me, "Please walk away." I looked at them disapprovingly, and replied that I wouldn't. The team did make me a bit nervous, because of the village we were in and its reputation, but I tried to contain my fear. I asked the children if they would like to walk with me for a while. They were hesitant, so I said goodbye and moved to continue my walk, but suddenly I found them running after me. When they reached me, they walked quietly by my side. For a moment, I felt scared. I looked ahead of me and saw that Younes had walked further ahead, but suddenly found Osama walking by my side. I looked at him, trying to show that everything was fine, so he moved a few steps ahead, but kept walking at our pace.

I asked the boys their names, and then I asked them if they wanted to know mine. I also asked their ages, and learned that the eldest was eight and the others were between five and seven. They were all wearing grey or beige jilbab and leather slippers on their feet. We talked about their school and they told me that we would walk past it, and when we did they pointed it out to me. It consisted of a small building and a small playground. They also pointed out to me the youth center they played football and karate in, telling me that these were the only two sports available there.

The police securing our walk suddenly came over to us and, from their car, asked the kids to return to their village, but the kids refused. Osama told me that he was afraid that they wouldn't be able to get back if we walked much further, but I disagreed. We were walking in a straight line, so they wouldn't have any difficulties navigating their way back. Yes they were between five and eight but they were not like the children that are raised in towns or cities. These children went everywhere on foot, from the time they had started walking, and even before that they would crawl all over the place. In Aswan, I had seen a three-year-old child riding a tricycle for the first time, and his father stood beside him, clapping joyfully and crying out that his child had just driven for the first time.

It was getting dark and suddenly the children passed the street, climbed into a tuk-tuk, and left . . . without saying goodbye. Osama immediately relaxed and started to walk slower, at his own pace.

The plan on this day was to walk 42 km. We had done 27 km so far, and had 15 remaining and it was already around five-thirty. One of the ladies from the Red Cross had a nine-year-old relative with her, who wanted to walk with me. She wasn't wearing suitable shoes or clothes for the walk, but she had a strong will, so she even walked at my pace. I asked her about her school, and she told me that it was very bad. Everything they studied she had already studied before, and she couldn't make friends. I asked her why that was and she told me that she had lived in Kuwait all her life and that they had only moved to Egypt a year ago.

She told me that she had liked the school in Kuwait and that she liked science and math, but that here it was dull and her classmates were dull as well. "I don't like them and I don't like the way they talk," she said.

I felt pity for the girl. The move represented a very big social and cultural change, from a Gulf country to a village in Upper Egypt. Without a doubt, she would have had much more exposure than her classmates and probably more than her teachers as well. I asked her if she had brothers and sisters and she said, "I have a younger sister. She is still a baby, and my mum is always with her. I feel that she has forgotten about me. But my dad plays with me sometimes."

The sun had set by this time, and it was getting cold. I started to put my jacket on and asked her if she had one, but she told me that she was not cold. I held her hands and felt they were a bit cold, so I kept them in mine to warm her up. Younes was still ahead but I knew that Osama and Ahmed were behind us and I hadn't seen them in a while. The girl and I walked a bit faster to catch up with Younes. I get bored walking at night and I wanted to hear some of his music to help kill the time and dispel the feeling of loneliness. I asked him to raise the volume a bit, but he couldn't because the battery was low. He told me to come and walk beside him, so we could hear better and we did so. But the girl felt reticent about walking beside him and I didn't want her to walk in the road, with the cars driving past, so we walked in front of him. We couldn't hear the music, so I decided to make my own.

We entered a new city, Dishna, which is the fourth biggest in Qena with around 410,000 inhabitants in 2015. Dishna means launch, and it is said that it was named Dishna because it was from this location that the French had launched their ships into the Nile during the French campaign in Egypt. Early modern Egypt was under occupation by different empires: The Ottoman occupation, the French occupation (1798 - 1801), and the British occupation. We became completely independent in 1922.

It was a very busy city, with a two-way street running through it, peopled with tuk-tuks and cars and many people walking in both directions.

The train station was on our left, and many buildings were on our right. I started reading all the signs we passed and all the shop names, saying anything that came to my mind. I wanted to distract us a little, as the girl was cold and quiet beside me, and so was Younes. Suddenly, we found ourselves in the middle of nowhere. We had left Dishna, and to our right and left were fields. The street lights were very low and before we knew it, Younes' speakers were entirely out of charge. We had 4 km left for the day and we had to continue the walk.

Younes was looking around all the time to make sure we were safe, but there was no one with us on the road and we were still in a dangerous area. We called Osama and Ahmed to check on them; Osama told us that some people had threatened him for money but he was fine, and Ahmed was still behind, but the support car was following him.

We were 1 km away from our finish point and we didn't know where Mohamed was. I called him and he told me that he was making his way to us. Younes didn't like that; we couldn't just stand in the street waiting in such an area. We would be targets for anyone who wanted to threaten us. People from the Red Cross were approaching us, so the situation was getting better but still, we knew that when we finished there would be no car for us to sit and wait in. I called Mohamed again and he sounded relaxed; he wasn't far away.

Forty-two km had been completed by eight-thirty pm. I pinned the location on Google Maps, then we saw that Mohamed had arrived. By this point, Younes was feeling more relaxed and had gone to pee in the bushes. I was cold, so I said goodbye to the girl and climbed into the car and she went over to the Red Cross car. Osama reached us and I asked him what had happened.

"It was dark," he told me, "and suddenly four kids appeared from nowhere and asked for money. I was startled for a moment, then I yelled at them. They had glass bottles, so they threw them at me and ran off."

I asked if he was injured and he said no, then continued, "But all they wanted was one pound."

We laughed.

We were ready to go back when Ahmed reached us, and during the car ride we got the hint that Ahmed was really not feeling well. Younes also mentioned that he had a problem, a very big blister was irritating him. After having seen Osama's blisters, it sounded as though Younes' injury was really minor, so we took it lightly. I was so tired that I slept almost half of the car journey, and when we reached the hotel at ten-thirty, I was barely able to get out of the car. I had a quick bite in the restaurant, then headed to my room. We were due to leave the hotel the next day, for a new hotel in a new city that I had never visited before.

Day 10
QENA
Qena, Dishna
42km – 8h 37m

Qena

Day 11

I HAD BEEN waiting for this day for the past three days. The Red Cross team told me that in Qena governorate there was a city called Nagaa Hamadi on the west bank, and that just adjacent to it on the east bank we would see the best scenery on the road. Every day, I told Younes that this was what I was waiting for, and when he planned the route I made sure that it would be on our way.

We were ready with our luggage at five-thirty am in front of the rooms, waiting for the shuttle bus to take us to the hotel lobby. No one had breakfast in the restaurant that day, as we had started to depend more on breakfast boxes and eating during our breaks or while walking along the way. We got to the lobby at six, the cars were loaded and we left at six-thirty, leaving the support team to arrange the check out for everyone.

At eight-thirty we started the walk, and I was extremely excited. The previous day, we had been scared when we got to our finish point, but in the morning light everything was beautiful—greenery and blue canals. But we weren't all as excited: Ahmed wasn't feeling well at all. But we wouldn't know that until later.

Each of us was walking with members of the Red Cross, talking about nature and the tribes that lived in this area. There are several tribes in Qena, and the three most prominent, with the largest status, are called El Ashraf, Arab, and Howara. They compete over who can secure the most chairs in Parliament, and whomever wins brings prestige to the whole tribe. On a social level, intermarriage between the tribes is forbidden, especially by El Ashraf. Their members consider themselves to be the best ethnic group because they are reportedly descendants of the prophet Mohamed, so they don't want to be mixed.

Among the Red Cross team that day, there was a girl called Sohad. We walked together for a while, and she told me about her life. She had her miseries, but she was trying to get over them. She didn't walk with me for long, then she disappeared into the Red Cross car.

We were approaching Nagaa Hamadi, and I could see a range of mountains looming ever closer and bigger. The road curved, palm trees to the right and left offering an intriguing glimpse of what might be hidden at the very end. Because of my eagerness, I was walking quickly at the very front of the group, until I got a call from Younes.

He was a hundred meters behind me and he told me with urgency, "Come back—Ahmed is not okay."

I paused my tracking application and hurried back. I found Ahmed in the car, with Osama and Younes standing at the window beside him. I sat on the front seat, and listened to Ahmed as he told us he wouldn't be able to continue. His Achilles' tendon was hurting him badly, and he couldn't stand on his feet anymore. We all told him that his safety and well-being were the most important considerations, with Osama adding, "I may follow you soon."

I was starting to get really worried, but this time my fears were not for me, but for the guys. I started observing how they walked and checking on them periodically. More accurately, I was checking on Younes and, at the end of the day, checking on Osama. Younes only ever had two responses: either, "I'm fine, I know my body well," or, "I have a very big blister—it's almost as big as my toe." I sensed that both were exaggerations, but anyhow I knew that he wouldn't get annoyed if I checked on him every now and then.

But Osama was a different story. Before the trip, we had gone to do a fitness check and the doctor had told us that between me and Osama if anyone was to walk the whole way, and anyone stop, Osama would be the one to stop. That got on Osama's nerves, and he said that the doctor was unprofessional and didn't know what he was doing. It was true that we didn't like the fitness tests that this doctor had done, and that we didn't consider his practice well organized. But, we had also undertaken stress tests and found these to be accurate.

Although I was the oldest in the team, my heart health and my stress resilience were much better than Osama and Ahmed's. This was especially the case for Osama, because the tests had said that his heart health was not very good and that he was easily stressed. But no one had expected that Ahmed would be the first to stop. The day after this day, I would see that Osama was in pain and would end up sending a message to Younes on WhatsApp, asking him to check on Osama. I knew that if I checked on him, his answer would have been that he was fine—even if he wasn't.

I had put my music on and resumed walking, and after another 4 km we found a gas station, with a shaded outdoor coffee shop just beside it. It had sandy ground, plastic chairs, and a wooden table. Lunch time was coming soon and the food was on the way, so we rested there.

The nine-year-old girl who had walked with us the day before turned out to have been in the Red Cross car all that time, but her shoes were torn. As she couldn't walk with us, she came to join us over lunch. I ordered coffee but there was only tea available, so the owner of the place went to buy coffee. When he returned, I told him that I wanted it with milk. Judging by his frustrated look, I understood that he didn't have milk, so I just took black coffee. While waiting for the food, Younes made himself comfortable, raising his legs on the chair, so his thighs were exposed. The girl looked at them, blushing, and couldn't take her eyes off him. It may have been her first time to see that much of a man.

The food arrived—once again, rice, vegetables, and grilled meat. I ate few spoonfuls of rice and a few pieces of meat, but couldn't eat more. As always, the guys ate most—if not all—of their food. After a two hour break, we were ready to continue our walk. While two hours may seem a long time to break for, they flew by. Every day after we had eaten, had a hot drink, searched for a place to pee, and sat raising our feet for a while, we found that we needed to get going. On this day, it was a little after three pm and we still had 24 km left. I was filled with excitement, knowing that we would pass the most beautiful places beside the Nile. More than this—this was the day that we would cross the Nile on foot!

At our starting point, we became three not four. But we knew that Ahmed would rest for a day or two and rejoin us. At the count of one, we resumed our walk. We were already beside Nagaa Hamadi, and the road was a narrow, two-way road, with palm trees on both sides. There was a series of huge yellow mountains just to our right, the mountains of the Red Sea, and the Nile was wide and sparkling just on the left. It was so peaceful that I felt as though I was walking in a picture or as

Younes had described it later, it felt as though we were being hugged by the mountains and water.

We then started getting excited in anticipation of the next big thing: crossing the Nile. I saw the bridge that we were going to walk over, and looked over at Younes with a smile. When I pointed at it he couldn't see it at first, but as we got closer he did. We played a game of guessing how many kilometers were left before we reached the bridge. I guessed two, one of the men from the Red Cross guessed one, then another said that the farthest the human eye can see is 5 km, so it must be 5 km away. I don't know if that's true, though.

We continued walking and after 3 km, we reached the start of the bridge and waited for Osama. Ahmed was in the support car behind, so Younes called him to come and be with us for this moment. I felt excited that we would be walking across the bridge all together, but I would never have thought of asking Ahmed if he could walk with us. And, truthfully, I was a bit startled. Anyone in Younes' shoes could have been forgiven for thinking that now life was being fair. Why Younes didn't hold a grudge, I couldn't say.

Ahmed was able to join us, and the four of us started walking to the entry point for the bridge. Arriving there, we found a security checkpoint, and because we had all the permits needed for the walk, they allowed us to cross the bridge on foot. The reason for the many checkpoints on the road is that Egypt is currently under a "state of emergency," as it has been since 1981, and since then it keeps extending it for months and years. But the only way it affected us was just by slowing us down. The bridge was 1 km, meaning that this was the width of the Nile at this spot. It consisted of a two-way road, with a wide wall on both the right and left sides. The wall blocked the view a bit, so Osama climbed it. Though this wasn't legal, we all did the same and walked along in a straight line with the Nile beneath us. The videographer went into the truck of the police car, securing us, to shoot the walk, and he kept ordering the driver of the police car to slow down or to go faster or to go a bit to the right or to stop for a while. The police literally became servants to the nation as their slogan say.

That fifteen minute walk was relaxing and purifying. It was five pm, just before sunset and we walked above the Nile. It was so blue on our left and the sky was orange on our right, and flocks of birds were flying together over the Nile. I walked at the front because I was the shortest, then Osama, then Younes, then Ahmed. The moment we stepped off the bridge, the sun set completely.

Osama, Younes, and I walked together. "I felt that I was walking in a dream. It was amazing," Younes expressed.

Osama gave him an indifferent look and replied, "It was a normal walk, the same as any other walk."

I looked at Younes, amazed, and told him that the timing was so strange, as the sun set the moment we finished and we were able to witness the sunset over the bridge.

"Yes," he answered, "if we'd planned it, we wouldn't have been able to arrange for it to happen like this." It was such a fulfilling moment; maybe not for Osama, but Younes and I had smiles on our faces.

I looked at the back and found Ahmed still walking with Hamdy. I told him that he would better rest if he would want to be better soon, however, he replied that he was okay and Younes then told me to leave him do what feels right for him. But it wasn't too long until he went back to the car.

There were two villages that we needed to walk through before our day was over. We passed Ar Rizqah then Abu Tisht, a bigger village with a train station. The moment we entered Ar Rizqah, the police securing us disappeared and that was not a good sign. It was night, and we were walking along a narrow two-way street, busy with tuk-tuks and people, kids on bikes and running around. Usually busy areas are safe, as no one will harm us with everyone watching, but it can be very irritating to have to traverse lots of people and vehicles when we were so tired.

The kids were running around us and following us on their bikes. They were taking photos and videos of us and behaving in a threatening way. The next village was on the agricultural road and they told us that it was not safe to walk there in the dark. They told us that butchers would come and kill us. That idea is funny to think about now, but then we were heading towards the unknown. More than anything, I was getting tired. My feet were hurting badly; it was like having fire in my shoes. We had a few kilometers to walk to get out of that village, so I wanted to prepare Younes for the fact that I would need a rest. We were all walking together as a group: me, Osama, Younes, and the Red Cross team.

I looked at Younes and told him in a low voice, "I need a rest soon."

"Okay, when we get out of here," he replied.

The moment we left the village, we found that the kids were right. It was dark and dismal but I had to stop, I couldn't stand on my feet anymore.

"I need only a three minute rest," I told Younes.

He wanted us to keep walking because he feared that the experience we had had the day before could be repeated, or that we might even experience something worse. But I didn't wait for his consent and headed to the back of the car, opened the door, sat on the trunk, and took my shoes and socks off to air them.

The children followed us and I found one of them taking a video of me. I told Osama about this and he immediately went over to the child and took his phone for a moment, before returning. By that time, my feet were better and I had my socks and shoes on. We resumed the walk and I asked Osama what had happened.

"I asked him to delete the video but he refused," Osama told me, "so I took the phone and reset it to factory settings." We laughed out loud, as he continued gleefully, "That kid thought that he could outsmart me!"

The kids left to go back to their village and the police appeared.

Osama asked them, "Do you always come late, like in the old Arabic movies?"

We all laughed, including the police officers, who answered, "The movies only mimic reality." That became our joke for the last 8 km, to finish our 42 km for that day.

It was six and 8 kilometers meant two hours. I could walk for another two hours. Yes, I was in pain, but I didn't feel that that would be a problem. It wasn't the best walk; again, we were walking along a narrow, two-way road in the dark. We walked in a straight line at a moderate pace. In the last kilometer, I walked a bit faster then waited for Younes when only 200 meters were left, because it was his watch that determined when we had completed the distance. At eight, we reached Ar Rawatib village, and that was our stop for the day.

I sat in the front seat of the car, with Osama and Younes in the back. I took off my shoes and socks and apologized for the smell. Younes quickly told me that we all smelled bad and Osama objected, "No I don't . . . Really, have my feet ever smelled bad?"

I answered him, "I didn't notice, Osama."

"I apply henna on my feet," he continued, "which absorbs any smell. And there's something else that I do every night: I order two cups of hibiscus and I soak my feet in them."

We were too tired to have a serious conversation, but I thought about Mohamed. After such a long day, he had to drive us a long way, with the smell of feet, socks, shoes, and sweat.

We arrived in Sohag. It was ten-ten pm and as we were waiting in the lobby for the support team to check us in, I saw that there was a new girl. Sally had been replaced! I had tried to call Sally the previous day, but couldn't get through to her. How could they already hire a new girl? I asked myself. We were asked to go to the reception desk to sign ourselves in, then I took my key and went to my room.

We were staying at the Nile Elite hotel, which is a three-story standing boat. It seemed as though it had once been a hotel for the elite, but not anymore. The stairs were spiral, and I carried my bag up them to my room, on the first floor. There was a long corridor on the left, and another on the right. My room was the last room on the right and the guys were on the left.

I went inside. There was a very narrow corridor and the bathroom door on the left, then a very small room ahead, with a low ceiling. I put down my bags and checked the bed sheets, which were clean, went to the bathroom and found that everything was clean there too. I returned to the room, closed my eyes and fell onto the bed. But I didn't sleep; we still needed to eat.

I was so hungry that even though I felt that I couldn't get up, I forced myself to. I went to the lobby, Younes was there and we were waiting for the rest of the team. It was already eleven and I just couldn't wait anymore. We started calling everyone then, to suggest that anyone who was ready come with us to the restaurant just in front of the boat. It was a Syrian restaurant which was said to be the best in town: The Damascus Corner. The waiters prepared a long table for us. I put my head on the table and closed my eyes until we got the menus, then it took fifteen minutes for all of us to order. I ordered two sandwiches and was only able to eat half of one of them. I took the other one and returned to my room before everyone else.

This was the first day I went to bed without a shower. I could barely stand. "Tomorrow I am going to call Sally," I thought, then I drifted into sleep.

Or so I wished. This night turned out to be one of my worst. My feet were on fire, and my legs were hurting all the way from the top down. My brain was feverish. I was in a very small room, which seemed to be drawing in on me, tighter and tighter. The longer I was there, the more suffocated I felt.

It took a huge mental effort for me to resist this feeling of suffocation.

I remembered when I went to Hong Kong for a vacation. My budget was tight and the hotels were expensive. I stayed in a room with private bathroom for 50 USD per night, which was in a skyscraper with six elevators. Each floor had twelve apartments and each apartment had many rooms. When I entered my room, I had to roll my luggage on its side because the corridor was so narrow. After two steps, there was a bed which had a small room to store the luggage below it. And the bed was almost the size of the room. There was a TV hanging on the wall, a fan, and an AC, all suspended on the walls above the bed. And if you moved two paces to your side, you would find the bathroom door. Stepping into the bathroom was the only move you could make. Using the toilet, you sat; showering, you stood and it was just above you, with the sink in front of you. The room had everything I needed, arranged in a compact way, but it was only a place to sleep.

At Nile Elite, at least there was some space to move around and a window. I opened the curtains and found that my room overlooked the Nile. "Given that I cannot even stand, or bring myself to turn to my right or my left, why would I want a bigger room?" I said to myself.

Then the pain started to fade and I started to fade as well, until I was asleep.

Day 11
QENA
Deshna, Nagaa Hamadi, Ar Rizqah, Abu Tisht
42km – 8h 50m

Day 12

THE PREVIOUS DAY, we had finished eating and gone to bed late. It was one of the toughest nights that I experienced—if not *the* toughest. We were supposed to have breakfast at seven am and I woke up at six but kept hitting the snooze button on the alarm until I finally got up at six-thirty. I usually took my showers before going to bed but on that previous day I simply hadn't been able to stand on my feet. So I had my shower after getting up, and got dressed in a very lazy manner. I went to the restaurant at seven-fifteen to find Younes and Hamdy already there and almost finished with breakfast. I only had a Nescafe, as there was no French coffee, and I ate some small pieces of the pastries at the open buffet while standing, to save time. Osama came a bit later, ate quickly and we hit the road. We had 68 km to travel in order to return to our starting point.

We started our walk a few minutes before nine. It was our first day after crossing the Nile, and we were on the west bank, still in Qena. A small canal was on our right and fields or houses were on our left all the way. After a few kilometers, I found Osama looking like he was in pain. As he walked, he was looking straight ahead, clenching his jaws. I wanted to suggest to Younes that he check on him, knowing that if I asked him he would immediately say he was all right without stopping to reflect. I sent Younes a text, asking him to check on Osama, then I walked a few steps ahead to give them space to talk freely. After few moments, Younes came over to me and told me that he had asked Osama indirectly how he was and that he was fine. I replied that I just felt that he was hurting and he didn't want to tell me.

"But yesterday he told Ahmed that he might follow him soon, so he is being open about it," Younes told me.

"Yes, I was astonished by that," I replied.

Ahmed rested in the morning and then went to the doctor at night. The doctor instructed him to rest for three days. However, Ahmed said that he didn't want to return home with an injury because he would like to resume his training one week after we were back. Ahmed undertakes triathlon with the national team and he was training to break the Egyptian record by the end of the year, or so he said. So he decided that if he wasn't feeling well after those three days, he would walk only 10 km per day with us, from then on. Younes wished him a quick recovery to be able to rejoin us soon, and I told him that the most important thing was that he take care of his health, so he would be well. As I said this, I wasn't sure whether he was really keen to continue the walk with us.

For the next five days, we didn't see Ahmed except at lunch or dinner and everyday he appeared with a look of despair. At first we were sympathetic and asked about his feet every time. But after a while, I personally didn't care. The three days of rest that were recommended by the doctor had passed and he didn't say a word about completing the challenge, nor did he come to walk the ten kilometers per day he had said he would. Pushing oneself is part of the challenge. The first thing he did after his fight with Younes, over who was truly the leader, was to state that he didn't want to be part of the team and he was going to quit. Moreover his first injury was trivial. I mean we were attempting to walk almost 1000 km and endurance athletes don't pay attention to such injuries, but they push themselves despite them. To succeed in a challenge one needs determination and willpower.

The road was a narrow, two-way road; our support cars blocked half of it and, whenever that happened, we felt responsible for blocking the way. I was walking in the front, with Osama and Younes just behind me when suddenly I saw a police car travelling at an unreasonable speed. It passed me by, and then I saw another car coming after it, moving at the same speed. Then I heard a crash. I looked behind me, terrified that I would see someone from the team hurt. Younes and Osama were okay, and we ran towards the accident to find that three cars had clashed. The car speeding after the police car had hit two vehicles coming from the opposite direction, and the driver was hurt.

One of the vehicles was a microbus, with many passengers in it, and the other was a car that was dented, but whose driver wasn't hurt. Our cars and teams were fine. All the team went to get the driver out of his car. I went to see the women in the microbus, one of whom had an injury on her lips; it was cut and bleeding. I asked Mohsen to help her; although he is a physiotherapist he had an emergency kit that enabled him to treat minor wounds. She was initially reluctant because he was a male doctor, but we told her that he would simply apply some antiseptic. Then Younes came calling for me to resume the walk; there was nothing else we could do there.

We had entered the governorate of Sohag, and the police there were very strict in providing us with security and protection. I was walking at the front when I found an officer getting out of the police car and walking next to me, with a rifle by his side, ready to shoot. The police car kept driving a little way ahead of me, presumably to remain in close proximity, for my safety. But honestly, I was shocked and felt imprisoned. Over the past eleven days, I had been walking freely on the road, greeting anyone I wanted to and talking with children, listening to music, and dancing with nature. Now, it was as though my movement had been restricted and my freedom taken away.

For the whole duration of our twenty-four day walk we were escorted by different groups of policemen, often officers sitting in trucks holding their rifles. The less high-ranking policemen were usually more relaxed and less serious. Many officers asked us about the purpose of the walk and few could see the relation between undertaking a sports challenge and raising awareness about social issues. Generally, I think we were seen in the early days as a group of spoilt kids who were simply taking up their time and energy; they could have been sitting in their offices otherwise. But starting from Sohag the police were more serious in their approach to us, and so was the vibe of the cities and the people we encountered.

I looked towards the back and saw Younes walking with Hamdy and other people from the Red Cross. I didn't want to wait for them, because I didn't want to walk with Hamdy and this made me feel more imprisoned. I couldn't even move to the back. But I did slow down a bit, so I wouldn't be walking right beside the officer with a rifle. Then I found a man from the Red Cross approaching me.

"What's your name?" he asked.

I told him my name.

"Where do you live?"

"Cairo."

"You know, I will move to Cairo soon."

"Why is that?"

"Just circumstances," he answered, vaguely. "Give me your number to check on you when I am in Cairo."

I looked at him, speechless at this strangeness and the audacity of his request. The same question kept running around my head: who did this man think he was. I had met him a minute earlier, and he felt he had the right to ask for my number. I couldn't take this as well.

"You can take the numbers of the guys at the back," I finally replied.

I wanted to walk away but I didn't know where I could go. Was it better to move towards the rifle, or to go to the back and be faced with Hamdy's unwanted attentions? I slowed my pace even further, and I think the Red Cross man started to understand that I didn't want to walk with him. I just felt desperate.

Seeing me turn around, Hamdy noticed that I wasn't well and I found him by my side a while later.

"The accident in the morning has put us all in a bad mood," Hamdy said.

"Yes," I agreed.

He kept talking about different topics to try to lighten the mood, but I was quieter than usual. I felt suffocated and I didn't want to talk much, to avoid crying, but my voice kept cracking. Finally, Hamdy left to go and arrange lunch and the police officer got tired and went to sit in his car, and the intruder from the Red Cross went to walk with other people, and at last I had the chance to shed few tears.

Still, in the middle of the day, a girl from the Red Cross got out of the car to come and walk with me. Talking with her was pleasant and gave me hope in the women of Upper Egypt. She had many aspirations and was involved in many activities. She likes drawing, she is in a drama group, she travels locally whenever possible, and she volunteers with the Red Cross. I felt that I had met my soul mate: I draw, I have tried acting, I love traveling and whenever there is a suitable volunteering activity I join it.

But where we were very different was that I like sports and play them whenever possible. She told me that she enjoys them too, but that she doesn't practice regularly. When I asked her why, she told me, "I don't want to be thin, I look more beautiful when I am curvy." This took me by surprise. I had thought she was someone who rebelled against the categories and boxes that we, as women, are put in. I had seen her as ready to push back against societal norms and the way we are "supposed" to think. But apparently that idea was very farfetched.

Throughout the journey, I kept meeting women and found, contrary to my expectations, that several of them were doing their Masters degrees or preparing their PhDs. Though I was surprised, I came to learn that, in some areas, the better the woman's degree, the more desirable a husband she can marry.

We reached Bardes, a village in Sohag, and it was time to take a break. The village was teeming with shops and cafeterias, and cars passed in both directions on the road. Funnily enough, it is said that the name Bardes comes from the word paradise, yet we couldn't find anywhere suitable to eat.

Because we didn't know where to eat, I went over to Younes and suggested with a smile that we eat at the police truck.

He replied, "If possible, why not?"

To be honest, we were both like children who wanted to look inside the police car and were using our cunning to work out how we could do that. So we put our request to the police. At first they said it was possible, but then suddenly we found tables and chairs appearing from nowhere and being placed on the sidewalk. The police had talked to the owners of the coffee shops in the street, and they provided us with chairs and tables. The food was the usual: grilled meat and chicken, rice and vegetables. We sat on the chairs and tables on the sidewalk, eating with our hands, as people walked in front of us and cars spluttered fumes all over us. After eating, we found that the police had organized for us to go and wash at the tourism office next to where we were seated. Then we were ready to get going again.

After a few kilometers, we were out of the main village and we found that our surroundings were quieter and more ordered, as we passed huge swathes of greenery and small villages every now and then. We walked together this time and I was feeling much better. We talked about mental and physical stress.

"Does physical stress affect mental stress or the other way around?" I asked Younes.

"They both affect each other," he replied.

"When I am physically stressed, I find my stress resilience is lower," I said.

"Also when you are mentally stressed, you may not be able to perform at your best, physically," Younes replied.

We were silent for a while, then Younes looked at Osama and told him, "A friend is telling me that there's an application that will allow us to earn bitcoins with every step we take."

"We would make a fortune then," Osama replied. They continued to talk about that topic with a blithe unawareness that I might know anything about cryptocurrency.

The previous night hadn't only been bad for me—all the support team had complained about the size of the hotel room we had stayed in. I had suffered the day before, but I hadn't complained and nor had Osama or Younes. Ahmed had then called to inform me that we would change hotels, but my luggage was unpacked. Ahmed told me that he could pack it for me, but I answered absolutely not; he was going to pack for the guys but it wasn't right for him to pack my personal things for me. I called Hamdy and he told me that he would not check out for me and I would have to do so myself after the day's walk.

Night had fallen and the road took us left, then right, as we walked between the fields for two hours. We were stressed, walking in a straight line along yet another narrow two-way road. The Red Cross kept trying to walk beside us but I repeatedly asked them to walk either in front of or behind us to avoid accidents.

The stress and boredom I felt on this road, along with the pain in my feet, made me walk quickly to try to finish as soon as possible. In the daylight, seeing the changes in sunlight and scenery and passing people and cars in the street made us feel that time was passing and we were progressing, but at night, every hour was like the one before: dark and quiet. To feel some small sense of progress, I would check how many kilometers were left and I even started counting the light poles we passed, as a means of counting down the time remaining. So I would check the distance between the poles, and divide it by the distance remaining to know the number of light poles left and start counting the poles accordingly.

We got in the car and headed back to the city, Sohag. Before going to the new hotel, we passed a fish restaurant, Ahmed Osman Fish, to have our dinner. The police officers were having dinner with us and the guys ordered for them. We ate rice, a popular Egyptian soup called molokia, seafood pasta and fried fish, which was all okay but the food took far too long to be served, and we were starving and exhausted when it came. I ate less than half of it, then was full and we headed to the hotel.

We would need to pass the new hotel to get to the old one. I told Mohamed to drop the guys off and then he could take me to the old one to pack, but he couldn't stop so they came with me. The guys stayed in the car and I told them that I would just run in for ten minutes. I went and packed quickly and when I returned Younes was gone; he had decided to walk to the new hotel. It took three minutes by car and when we arrived, I was carrying my bags inside when, out of the blue, I heard Younes's voice from behind me, "Do you need help?"

I looked at him and he smiled winningly.

"How do you still have the energy to smile?" I wondered. I thanked him and carried the luggage inside.

After doing the check-in process, I had to carry the bags up one floor. I stood with one medium sized bag, a laptop bag, backpack, and hiking bag, looking at the stairs and trying to figure out how I could carry them all up. I had just started organizing them when I found Younes by my side, asking again if I needed help. I could have used some help but I said no thank you again.

He remained by my side, standing there and looking at me, and then told me, "You are strong."

I considered this a compliment, but I wasn't sure if it was meant that way or not. I was still struggling with my bags, with Younes there beside me, when Mohsen came and saw the mess I was in. He too offered help and I said no thank you to him as well, but he didn't wait for my consent, and went ahead and carried some of my bags up anyway.

The new hotel was another boat hotel, called Nile Story. My room was bigger than the previous one had been, but honestly I liked it less. The sound of the generator was too loud and the bathroom wasn't clean. I asked the people working in room service to come and clean it, and it took them a long time to come and I was fighting not to fall asleep. When the person working in room service arrived, he told me that he was the only one on duty. I felt sorry for him but I also wanted a clean bathroom, so he went to get the cleaning products and I felt a bit better.

Before I threw myself into bed I received a message on my phone. "When I said you were strong, I wasn't being sarcastic, just in case you misinterpreted."

"I didn't . . . but I hope it's a good thing! Being a woman . . ."

"Absolutely . . . you are very determined and have strong will power . . . It's great."

"Thanks!"

I thought a while before writing the last thanks. I didn't know how should I feel or react. Younes had shown great strength, especially mental strength, so that accolade coming from him must really be good, I thought. But I was too tired to be able to process anything in my mind, so I just threw myself into bed and slept.

Day 12
QENA - SOHAG
Bardis
42km – 8h 43m

Day 13

I WAS FEELING much better physically and was able to wake up and move on time. We depended on having breakfast boxes to take away with us, because the restaurant in the new hotel didn't operate before seven. The day started quite lightly as we began our walk early in the morning, surrounded by a fresh breeze and nature. We then found that Mohamed and the support cars had disappeared, and we found them sitting at an open air restaurant com coffee shop, eating beans and falafel sandwiches and having tea. I went, greeted them, and quickly took half a falafel sandwich from Mohamed, without asking permission but flashing him a bright thank you smile. I left in seconds, and although they invited me to have more, I looked back and told them that I had enough and resumed my walk. Osama went and took a sandwich from Mimo. After taking the first bite, I knew that I was craving oriental breakfast. Most Egyptians eat beans and falafel for breakfast, or eggs with pastirma, and white cheese with baladi bread, which is whole wheat flat round bread, baked in a very hot oven. The food mostly made with a lot of margarine or it is deep fried. I had been eating cereal for breakfast for almost two weeks, and though I didn't find it tasty, it satisfied my hunger. As we continued walking, we found a coffee shop and stopped to buy coffee for me and Osama and tea for Younes. The coffee wasn't good, but at least it did its job.

We resumed walking and I asked Younes, "What does sport do to our bodies?"

"Walking such long distances can cause athletic heart syndrome," he replied.

"What does that mean?" I asked.

"The heart gets enlarged," he answered.

"And why is that bad?"

"It leads to slower resting heart rate."

"Isn't that better?"

"Yeah, in general it is, unless it causes problems. But it is also temporary; it doesn't stay with you after you stop exercising or decrease your rate of exercise."

"My average heart rate was 152 bpm on the first day, but today it reached 112 bpm and the maximum is 120 bpm."

"That means you're becoming fitter."

That day was the last that I wore the heart rate monitor. I found it very irritating, and putting it on and taking it off in the street wasn't always an option. I would usually put it on while I was in the car, before we started walking, and would then take it off during the breaks, but sometimes I couldn't because there was no privacy. On this day, I felt that I was okay and didn't need to keep tracking my heart rate.

"What about Ahmed's injury? Is it normal to get Achilles tendinopathy from walking?" I asked.

"He ran a lot during the walks and that may have caused the injury," Younes replied.

I liked the explanation that Ahmed's injury was because of his running, because I wanted to dismiss the idea that I might get injured because of the walk. Now I felt relieved and was able to put the idea of getting harmed at the end of the twenty-four days out of my mind. Yes, we never know what may happen, but at least I wasn't harming myself.

"And ah, what did you find out about the application that gives bitcoins with every step?" I asked Younes.

He was surprised at the question and answered lightly, "It requires different things to function properly, and it's a bit complex."

After my morning chat with Younes, I then had immersed myself in German until the Red Cross team arrived. One of the team assigned himself to be my follower—or, to be more precise, my shadow. If I took a step to the right, he came with me; if I took a step to the left, he imitated my movement. I was irritated, but not only because of that; I was irritated because I didn't like his energy. I didn't feel comfortable around him, so I wanted to keep my distance.

This, however, proved too difficult to do with this particular person. He had no respect for personal space. To be fair, I think he may not have realised that such a thing existed. He meant well, I know, but he was coming for two days—whereas I would be doing this for twenty-four days, without any respite. I would be walking, so I needed to feel good in the process. He was a kind man, however, and he spent some time explaining to me the geography of a particular area or the crops of a certain field. For some time, I was appreciative but then I reached breaking point. I needed to be alone.

I tried several times to walk faster, to be ahead of him, or to slow down. But nothing worked, so I suddenly started to run. I kept running for as long as I could, but still I felt his presence, I looked behind and saw that he was running after me.

I stopped and looked at him as he leant forward to catch his breath and I told him, in frustration, "You don't have to be with me all the time."

"I just want to protect you," he replied.

"There is a supporting car in front of me," I told him, "and another one just behind me. So please don't worry." I looked to the front and resumed my walk. This time he didn't follow, but I was so frustrated that I started crying anyway for just a couple of minutes to vent out.

After 10 km, we stopped for a short break. It was getting hot so I stood at the back of the car and changed my middle layer with a lighter one. My new routine was to wear the base layer, a light mid layer, a medium heavy mid layer and over everything the heavy jacket. Then after my body warmed up, I would take off the heavy mid layer, finally taking off the heavy jacket by noon. I would hide behind the door, changing, when one day I noticed Younes standing by the small opening of the door with his back to me. I wondered if he was doing this to avoid passers-by seeing me changing. After this, it became a habit that whenever I was changing behind the back door and he was around, he would act as a guard for me.

After a while the students from the Faculty of PE, Sohag University, arrived to join our walk. This was usually exciting; meeting local people and having a better understanding of the youth and their potential made me feel that I was seeing the future of Egypt.

The students arrived in their faculty bus. I peeked inside, looking for girls, but they were all boys. When they got off the bus, I was horrified: they were loud, boisterous, and unpredictable. Their teacher tried to bring them to order, but he couldn't. I stepped to one side and kept walking on my own, trying to avoid any interaction when I found

Osama by my side, shielding me from the students or just behind me, covering my back. He has been walking slowly at the back since the start of the day.

We couldn't cope with everyone and I didn't think there was any way I could have a respectful chat with the students; they seemed empty-headed to me, simply teasing one another and causing their teacher problems. To my surprise, that was the first time I saw Younes totally stepping out of his comfort zone, greeting the students warmly and walking in the middle, bro-hugging one or two of them.

However, after the 23 km walk, I got into the car to go for lunch. I was in the front seat when Osama came and stood by the door and tapped on my cap, teasing me. I looked at him, smiling, and I thanked him.

"For what?" he asked me.

"I know that I gave you hard time," I told him.

"Don't be silly," he replied.

I knew that I had, at various points, given him a hard time. He didn't have to be there for me but anytime he felt that I might have problems, he was. I remembered the first week of the challenge, when he couldn't even stand my presence around him, and I didn't understand *what* had changed but I was so glad that things *did* change between us.

I found that, after all, Younes had also been annoyed by the students. I hadn't noticed what had happened, but it seemed like that they had been challenging him. One of them came over to the car window, asking Younes I didn't hear what exactly, but it was just a childish challenge. We were all relieved when Mohamed drove us away.

I was always much more active after the lunch break than I was in the morning. My mood is always better, and so is my ability to perform physically. Osama had started walking before us, Younes counted down from three to one, and we started together. The scenery was getting less exciting for me—we had already passed most of the beautiful places, and walking along the west bank of the Nile meant that we were more likely to walk through cities and villages. The green fields were not wide areas of trees and crops, as before, but we walked instead past tall red brick buildings, in the middle of agricultural land.

That day didn't divide itself into two parts, as all the other days had. It consisted, rather, of a series of events. Before long, we had arrived in a village and again I found Osama by my side. Younes was around 50 meters behind, with the Red Cross team and a girl from the Red Cross came to walk with me, and we had a talk that I found very touching. Her name was Safa. I asked her what she found special about Sohag, and she answered me in song.

There is a song by Dalida called "Ahsan Nas." Dalida (1933-1987) was a model and actor born in Egypt to Italian parents and at the age of twenty-one she moved to France, where she started her singing career and became a well-known French vocalist and actress. After winning several awards in Italy and France she wanted to sing more profound lyrics and at age forty-six she sang six songs in Arabic, mostly about homesickness and celebrating the Egyptian nation. One of them is "Ahsan Nas." The song name basically translates as "the best people" and it is about the people of Egypt, and what distinguishes every city from the others. When it comes to Sohag, Safa told me that it is the city of singing. I asked her if she could sing and she said that she could, but she was too shy to sing in the street. She had deep, dark brown eyes with long black eyelashes and pink lips. She was dressed in black and it turned out that this was for a reason.

Safa left and the walk started getting more challenging; we passed through many villages and where the streets were narrow and busy with people walking or sitting in coffee shops on sidewalks. It was safe but not comfortable, so Osama came walking with me and his presence made it better. When we left the villages and walked through the fields we became more relaxed and talked about light topics, or Osama made jokes. When I wanted to go to the toilet, I told him that I would ask at a mosque we were walking past, so he rushed ahead of me to ask the men standing outside if I could go in, before confirming with me. This walk rebuilt our bond.

When night came, we all walked together. This day was the last day of all where I felt physically tired. I had got used to the 42 km walk, or the pain of a 42 km walk.

In the car, I told Osama and Younes about the man from the Red Cross who I had felt so stifled by that morning.

"Guys, the short guy from the Red Cross team really irritated me. He didn't do anything abusive, but just his presence annoyed me—and whenever I went to the right or to the left, he came after me. I had to yell at him." I was starting to be more expressive; over the past days I hadn't told anyone about my frustrations.

Osama didn't understand why I was annoyed, but Younes asked me, "You mean you felt negative energy?" I was a bit reluctant to say this, because I wasn't sure if I was exaggerating, but he had a positive tone in his voice, which encouraged me to speak truthfully and fully about my feelings.

"Yes," I replied.

"I also didn't like him," he said.

I was pleased that I wasn't alone in my feeling; at least I didn't feel that I was being completely unfair about the man. The problem was, people were treating us like heroes, which made us feel acutely the responsibility to follow a certain code of behaviour. We had to be welcoming, positive, social, elegant, and respectful.

We arrived at the hotel and, for the first time, Younes asked for Mohsen's help. He had a blister that was getting bigger every day, and it was irritating him but he wanted to wait until it popped by itself. However, it had reached a point where it hurt all the time and he was afraid that it would pop while he was walking in the day. Mohsen went to his room and popped it for him. The next day, Younes showed me a picture of how it had looked and I responded that it really looked as though he had another toe on top of his actual toe; he wasn't exaggerating after all. Osama had also asked for Mohsen to come over to his room, and from my room I could hear yelps of pain and laughter. Osama is ticklish, so he would both laugh when Mohsen massaged him and then sometimes yelp from the pain as well.

We were going to stay in another city the next day, Assiut, so I packed, took my shower, and slept like a baby.

Day 13
SOHAG
Sohag
45 km – 9h 10m

Sohag

Day 14

THE NEXT DAY, again only the three of us: Osama, Younes and I, all packed and ready, met at six-thirty and moved just after seven, reaching our starting point at 7:41. What I found really amazing and quite overwhelming was that no day was like the one before. When we reached the starting point, we found Momen from the Red Cross waiting for us enthusiastically.

The day before, we had had a very enthusiastic man from the Red Cross, Momen, who loved walking with us and felt the responsibility to be there for us all the time in case we needed to be rescued. The Red Cross teams usually joined our walks at ten or eleven am but Momen insisted on knowing at what time we were going to start, so he could walk with us from the very beginning. On that day, we had planned to start our walk at six, but we only reached the starting point at seven-forty. We found him waiting for us and were amused by his enthusiasm. He walked with me at the front and told me that he had arrived promptly at six and walked for 2 km, asking the people he met on the way if we had passed them. He thought that we would have started already. But everyone he spoke to had only just woken up and they couldn't give him a helpful answer. It wasn't until he spoke to a woman who had been working in front of her house since six, and she told him that she hadn't seen us walk past, so he took a microbus back and returned to the starting point to wait for us.

I felt a little overwhelmed to know that someone felt that what we were doing was so important, and that he so much wanted to be a part of it. We talked about his life in Sohag, and his studies, and he told me about the city, with its landmarks.

Then we entered Tahta City, still in Sohag governorate. This was the city that Refaa El Tahtawy, an Egyptian writer, teacher, translator, Egyptologist, and renaissance intellectual, had lived. To commemorate him, and his contribution, there was a big, white statue of him at the gates of the city.

Momen told me, "This is *haram*," (*haram* means forbidden, in a religious sense).

I looked at him and answered, "You are joking, for sure."

He gave me a serious look and told me, "No—statues and drawings are *haram*."

I quickly told him, "I am shocked by what you are saying, and I don't want to discuss this issue."

He replied, "But many scholars have said that it is forbidden."

"And others said that it is not, and again, I don't want to discuss such matters."

"But I studied Islamic Law and . . ."

I stopped him, saying, "Even if you studied Islamic studies for a few years, that doesn't make you a scholar, nor does it give you the right to tell me how I should think. And none of this would give you the right to deny me from having a different view to yours. And I told you several times that I don't want to discuss this issue, because I don't want to debate an issue that I am not also a scholar of. I have my references and you have yours. It is better not to debate, so please respect my choice." We stayed silent for few minutes, then we talked about other general things until we separated.

What I find especially sad about this is that the volunteers of the Red Cross should be better educated, given the organization they are representing, and its rules that no religious or political bias should be shown by a volunteer while they are on duty. We left Tahta and the fields that were to our right and left, with many buildings on the agricultural land. I wondered if they were legal or not but no one seemed able to answer my question.

We were supposed to be already in the next governorate, Assiut, and visit a youth center, but because we were behind, Osama suggested that since Ahmed was not walking, he went alone to represent us. This would become Ahmed's main task during the campaign: going to the youth centers and giving small talks about the challenge and the purpose behind our walk.

At the youth center in Assiut, one guy listening to Ahmed talk belittled the challenge, asking, "What is so hard about walking 42 km per day?"

Ahmed had replied, "Do you even know how far 1 km is?"

The guy, whose name was Maher, was provoked by this answer and snapped, "I'd like to walk with you and I'll show you that it's nothing!" We found him approaching us the next day.

Ahmed assigned himself another task as well: asking, during the breaks and at the end of each day, how many kilometers we had walked and then sharing this information in the WhatsApp group of the whole team. Every day he would announce "our" achievements, with a message like "Today—longest distance!"

After walking for 10 km, Younes got a call that there would be a group of young people waiting to surprise us further along the road. Then, we suddenly found a car approaching us and two guys emerged from it and came over to shake our hands and take photos with us. We were so taken by surprise that Younes and I weren't very friendly with them. The two men seemed very excited to see us. I didn't know who they were, but they turned out to be the managers of the next youth center.

Before reaching them, we stopped, waiting for Osama to be present with us. We looked behind us, but we couldn't see him; he was at the far back from the beginning of the day. Younes called him and he said he was on his way, but the road curved behind us, so we couldn't see how far away he was. We waited for ten minutes and still there was no sign of him.

Meanwhile, by this point, we were very close to the first youth center and it was clear that they could see us, so we had to go over to them. The boys waited in the street with huge posters welcoming and thanking us. We were treated as champions; they were cheering for us. I didn't know what to do, so I waved to them while walking along the other side of the street, but the center manager invited us in. I looked at Younes, who also looked a little overwhelmed, but he was faster than me in his reactions. He crossed the street and started high-fiving the boys. I didn't know if I could do the same or whether, as a woman, to do so would be against their culture. They were all boys—with no girls in the group whatsoever. So I followed behind Younes, cheering at them in return. The manager insisted that we go into the center. We didn't have much time, but Younes told me, "I cannot reject the invitation." I nodded in agreement and we walked in. We took a photo with the boys and managers and then Younes took a selfie with everyone and asked me to join. Then we wanted to leave; though they wanted us to stay more, we couldn't.

After 2 km, we found another youth center on the road and once again there were boys waiting for us, and the managers had flowers that they gave us in appreciation. We had to go in without Osama. I told Younes that we couldn't stay long and he agreed, but he was more relaxed than I was. We went inside and there was another crowd waiting for us; they too were all male. We were posing for a picture when suddenly a man gave Younes his baby to carry. This was a hilarious moment. Younes was standing in the middle of the photo, holding a baby. I stood beside him, with men and boys surrounding us. Then Osama caught up and was able to join us.

But Younes was the star of the picture. He was the focal point of attention, with everyone waiting for him and appreciating him. I didn't mind acting as a follower, but I wasn't sure whether they were simply clueless as to how to deal with a woman, as I wasn't sure what was acceptable in their culture. I thought that maybe deep inside they didn't want to cheer for me as much as they did for Younes, because that would mean acknowledging the capabilities of women, which they might not have been ready to do, especially in such a male-dominated society.

"We have to leave," I whispered to Younes, and immediately he became more assertive.

We started preparing to leave, although all the managers were insisting that we stay—intending to be hospitable. Younes gave them a firm look and refused to stay longer.

As we went out he told me, "We had to leave," explaining why he might have been a bit harsh, and again I nodded in agreement.

After another 4 km, there was another youth center on the way. When we arrived there, we found people standing with loud speakers and playing national songs to welcome us. We had to go in. Younes was taking a selfie and we all gathered around him. Again they were all male and I was the only female in the picture. Osama gave me a look that clearly showed he wanted me to be safe. The boys were surrounding me from all sides, Younes in the front taking the selfie and Osama came to stand beside me.

After few pics and lots of excited smiles from all the people around us to us, the food arrived and we wanted to sit somewhere to eat. Younes asked me if I would like to eat at the youth center, but I told him that I would rather not eat in front of them. He agreed and understood that it was because everyone was looking at us like we were celebrities and we wouldn't have been able to sit comfortably with everyone just watching us. Also, we didn't have enough food for everyone, and we couldn't eat in front of them without inviting them to join us. As we left the center, it was very clear that Osama wasn't feeling well.

We went out in search for a place to eat, finding a shaded cafeteria. As we sat there, I took off my shoes and raised my legs on a chair. And Osama did the same. We sat, waiting for food, and we could see Osama struggling to say something he didn't want to: "I may not be able to continue." Osama was at his peak, or perhaps it would be more accurate to say that he had surpassed his peak long ago.

This was shocking . . . and it was heartbreaking. Quitting is such a difficult thing to do—to the extent that, many times, we don't quit when it seems the obvious thing to do. I didn't expect that Osama would actually submit to pain. And to say out loud that he couldn't continue could only mean that his pain was absolutely unbearable.

We all were trying to act cool. I wasn't sure if I should say anything or not, feeling that he might be more sensitive to anything that I said, because of masculine pride. But I also felt very strongly that he had to stop. He had been in pain since almost the beginning of the challenge—it showed in his change in attitude during the first week, his constant requests for Mohsen's sessions, the limp in his walk, and the slow pace he maintained. He had a great many blisters all over the soles of his feet—how could anyone walk on these blisters day after day?

"Remember when you told Ahmed that if he didn't rest for a day, he would have to stop completely," I told him.

"He has to see a surgeon," Mohsen said. "The blisters in his feet don't look good and they keep recurring, which is very alarming."

"Your safety is the most important thing," we all told him.

He showed reluctance to stop and couldn't make a final decision. But when it was time to go, I wanted to make it easier for him though it wasn't easy for me.

I went out of the cafeteria to search for a toilet, and I found a fire extinguisher station and thought I might find one there. I told Younes that I would go there, but then I found Hamdy following me. I told him firmly that I didn't need company, and that I had entered hospitals, police check points, traffic stations, and many other places on my own. He smiled and replied that he still couldn't leave me alone.

We crossed the street and I was going to ask where the toilet was, but he had already done so, and I followed the directions that had been given to him. I went in and out and found him waiting for me. These things were too weird for my common sense to fathom. I had been walking large distances, along roads, up steep hillsides, down narrow streets, for fourteen days and here he was waiting for me so I didn't cross the road on my own! Anyway, it was three pm and we had to go. After we crossed the road I called to Younes from far away; I didn't want to go in and have say goodbye to Osama. Younes came, we went to the starting point and resumed our walk without Osama. He would have followed, if he could.

It was a sad beginning without Osama; we walked quietly for a while, with only Younes's music for company.

As we walked by Tima, a village in the north of Sohag, I saw two girls emerging from a small street and walking on the main road. It looked as though they were around seven and eight years old. One of them wore trousers and a t-shirt with long sleeves and a head scarf. The other was dressed the same, but wasn't covering her hair.

I asked them if they would like to walk with me, and they said they would. They told me that they had been at the public library, reading, and about how much they liked learning. I asked them what else they did during their vacation, and they replied that they just played in front of their house with their neighbours. I asked them if they had ever played sports before, but they hadn't. When I started to talk about our walking challenge, they were startled—especially the younger girl—and they asked me why I couldn't simply ride in the car. For her, our walking the length of a country and having an empty car follow us was illogical. I told her that, if I had been riding, I would not have met her. She smiled and then they had to leave, because they had reached their neighborhood. I was so happy that they were educated but I also wondered what type of books they had at the library. I was thinking of how the books could be enlightening or could hold them back.

As night fell, I was getting stressed. I told Younes that I was afraid we might have been the reason for the accident we had seen several days earlier, and I didn't want us to be the reason for another accident.

"I'm also irritated at walking in the dark down narrow streets and our cars blocking one third of the road. Probably we were the reason for the accident. If our cars weren't blocking the way, maybe the accident wouldn't have happened," he replied. But there was nothing we could do about it, except try to finish our day's walk as quickly as possible.

Meanwhile Osama had gone to see a doctor and I wanted to check on him. I sent to him a message before we finished the walk, asking how he was.

"I have bruises on my feet because of the blisters," he replied.

"Will you join us for dinner?"

"The doctor has forbidden me from going out . . ."

"Ok, take good care of yourself. I wish you a fast recovery."

"Don't let anyone call me; I don't want to talk to anyone."

"Whatever will make you feel most comfortable," I assured him.

It turned out that he had pus in his bruises that could become gangrenous if he didn't rest. I started to feel very down. The feeling of seeing a lion submitting to its enemy is very depressing. I felt so strongly that Osama's biggest fear was being defeated, as he always acts strong and even heroic sometimes, almost to prove to himself that he has some power. Being defeated by pain must have been killing him.

It was little after seven and we drove for almost an hour to reach the hotel. We went to have dinner at Spectra restaurant, a fusion cuisine. Our table was on the second floor, and I climbed the stairs with difficulty and sat down quietly. I went to the toilet and found Salma coming after me.

"If you need anything just let me know. I'm here to help you," she said.

I thanked her.

"I can also give you a massage if you need it," she continued.

"Ohhhh, that would be great," I replied jokingly. I realized that she was serious, but assured her that I didn't need special attention.

We went to a new hotel in Assiut, which was the guest house inside the University of Assiut, said to be the best in the city. We entered the university gates in our car and drove for a couple of minutes until we reached a huge building. It had a prominent entrance, with many steps. We took our bags and walked up, finding in front of us a huge hall with many doors. One of these led to the guest house. We went inside, and in the reception were two guys playing PlayStation; it was obviously a quiet time. We checked in and went to our rooms, which were big and clean but the bed mattresses was too hard. This was a real problem for me, because it made it difficult to roll onto my side. But still, eventually, I slept.

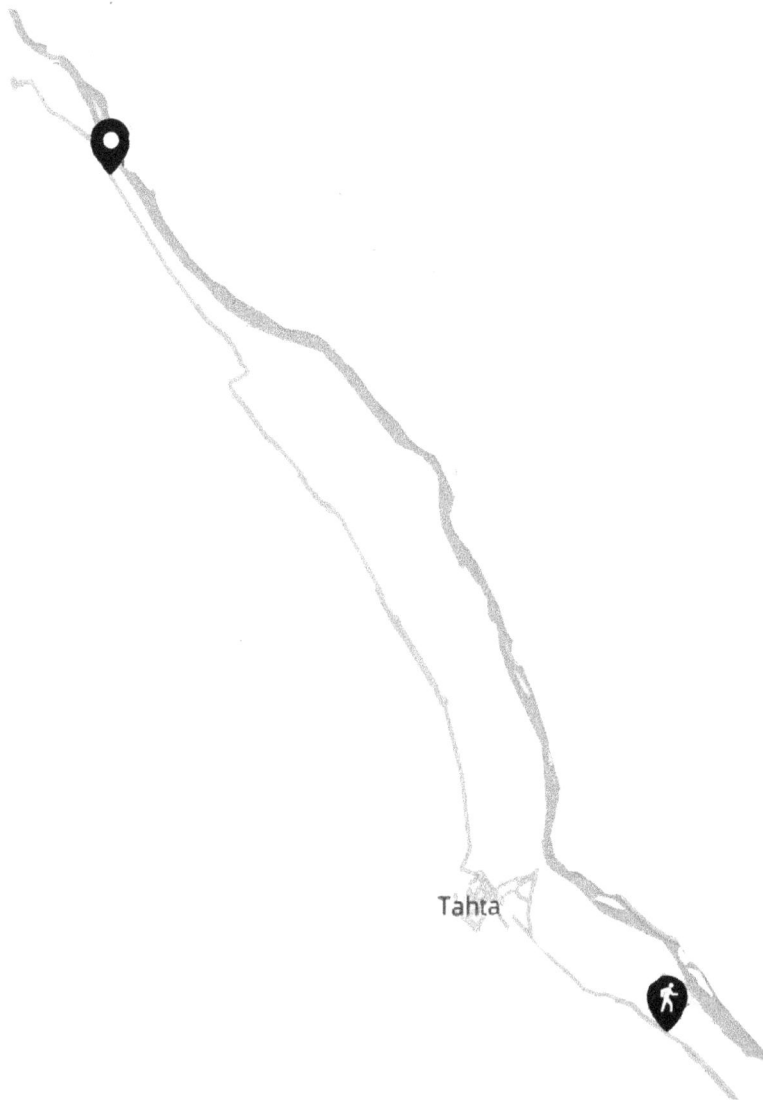

Day 14
SOHAG
Tahta
42km – 9h 28m

Tahta

Day 15

IT WAS ONLY Younes and I left on the road from our original group of four. At the end of the last day, we had just entered the governorate of Assiut, and were going to cross over the coming two days. Assiut is considered the beginning of Middle Egypt, so we had already crossed Upper Egypt! Changes in skin color and the openness of people's perspectives were becoming clear more and more frequently; this was a new milestone for us. Also it has the largest university in all of Upper Egypt, one of the best in the whole country.

We woke up at five-fifteen and moved at six. We started our walk together, passing along the agricultural road. We didn't see much greenery as we continued along the curving main road. There were two shortcuts that we could have taken, but Younes preferred that we take the main road, because we were less likely to encounter lots of traffic and people than if we passed through villages. The main road was also paved, which made it easier to walk on, but we were never sure of the state of the roads in the villages. I was fine with that decision, because the shortcuts would have saved us a distance of only 2 km at the most over the two days, so they really weren't worth it.

I had coffee at the hotel and Younes had his tea, so our basic needs had been met, and we carried our breakfast boxes as was our new normal. We walked 1 km, then we took a sharp left passing the first shortcut, and found that we were walking with many buildings on both sides of us. They looked as though they had emerged so organically; each had a different length and style, and it was clear that there was no plan whatsoever before building them.

That day, we met Maher, the guy who had challenged Ahmed at a youth center a day earlier. In the morning, around nine am, Younes and I were walking together and we found someone crossing the street to approach us. He told us that he had been at the youth center the day before, and he came to walk with us. We welcomed him. He started talking to me in German, but I kept replying in Arabic because Younes didn't speak German. I also found that I really didn't want to speak with him in German, feeling that he wanted to brag and I was perplexed that he had researched us before joining our walk and had known our backgrounds. Anyway, Younes had stepped back to let us hold the conversation in whichever language we liked.

I asked him where he had learned German and he answered that he had studied at a German center in Assiut. He had finished the first level but then they had replaced the teacher with one he didn't like, so he left. I suggested he look at online learning options, but he rejected the idea because he doesn't like studying by himself. I pressed him a little, emphasizing that maybe if he tried he would change his mind, because some of the courses are very interactive, but again he said no. To change the subject, I asked him why he had been so excited about walking with us and he told me about what had happened between him and Ahmed. Ahmed hadn't told us about it.

"So you are here to challenge us?" I asked.

"Ummm, not really, but walking 42 km per day is easy," he answered.

"Do you play sports?"

"I go running in the mornings and my friends can't keep up with me because I run such long distances," he answered.

"How far do you run?" I continued.

"Seven kilometers," he told me.

I replied, "That's really good."

"Yeah, I run frequently and my pace—both running and walking—is fast. And you're walking slowly!"

"When you're walking 42 km every day, you need to reserve your strength when you can. If you gave all your energy in one day, you might not be able to continue," I said, and we remained silent for a while.

Maher was on my left and there was a canal on my right. He kept moving closer to me incrementally, pushing me towards the canal. Every time I moved to the other side of him, he would once again move to my left and encroach on me—so I effectively felt trapped. I looked back and saw Younes, and tried to convey my need for help through my eyes. He came over and walked with us, so I could step back to take a break from Maher. I was happy to see them walking together, enthusiastically engaged in conversation. But after a while, Younes seemed to tire of Maher and I found myself walking with him once again. He repeated his story with Ahmed, and told me that he was waiting for him. I replied that Ahmed might not come that day for the walk.

Disappointed, he told me the story yet again.

I felt a little impatient and asked him, "Do you know how many times you've told me this story?" Without waiting for an answer I continued, "This is the third time and I really don't want to hear it again!"

He starred at me very weirdly and quickly defended himself. "I just feel provoked."

"That's not my issue," I replied. "If you want to walk with me then we can talk about pleasant things but if you're here to challenge Ahmed or to prove anything to him, that's not my business."

He looked even more disappointed. We were silent again but he kept gradually encroaching on my space as we walked.

Students from the Faculty of PE at Assiut University were going to walk with us; we anticipated that there would be girls along with the boys. This morning right before our departure from the university's guest house, we found girls standing in line waiting for something. Younes approached me saying, "They seem to be your friends for the day." The girls were around sixteen years old, and they looked athletic: all wearing sportswear and some of them were covering their hair and others weren't.

I went over to them, but they didn't know what I was talking about.

Asking their supervisor, I was told, "Yes, I heard about the walk. Other girls will join you—stronger than these ones," but no girls appeared. At ten, the boys arrived.

Younes and I split: in the beginning, I was in the front and he was in the middle of the group of boys. In the beginning I was reserved, but then I found that these boys were different than the ones we had met in Sohag, so I started to open up and talked with them. At first they too were reserved, but then they started to open up. They were amazed that I had been able to walk from Aswan—over 500 km. I asked them what they did and most of them replied that they were in their first year of college. One invited me to his wedding and I was startled.

"You're in your first year and you're getting married?" I asked.

"Yes," he replied with confidence.

"And how old is your fiancée?"

"She's two years younger than me."

So she was fifteen I thought. "And will you let her continue her education?"

"Yes," he replied reluctantly, "we agreed on that."

"And will you have children immediately after marriage?"

"No, we'll wait until she finishes school."

"But you don't use methods of birth control." It was a statement, rather than a question.

"No, that was in the past, now it is more common to use them," he answered, and his friends agreed.

"And when you have children, how many will you have?"

He answered without hesitation, "five or six."

I was astonished; I had thought that this generation would be thinking differently about the challenges of population growth. "How are you going to raise them and feed them when you're still in your first year of college and you don't have a job?" I asked, realizing how naïve I sounded.

Another boy answered, "We are generous people."

I made a gesture to indicate that I didn't see the relation between my question and his answer, so another boy contributed, "All the family supports each other."

"Our uncles will offer support if anyone in the family needs it," chimed yet another boy.

Then the boy who was planning to get married told me, "My dad supports the whole family. My wife will move to our house and we will all eat and live together."

"And how do the family men support five or six children each?" I asked, thinking that if each person had five siblings and each sibling had five children, then the patriarch of the family would have thirty children to support—and then, if you added the parents as well, forty members of the family.

Another boy answered, "We have land, weapons, and opium."

I heard that and couldn't argue with them anymore. They were living a totally different life, governed by a system that was different from anything I knew.

I walked with some of the other boys and they told me that they had a camp at their college. They would sleep at midnight and wake up at six am. I asked them what they spent their time doing at night, and their answer was parties. At the party, each of them would show off a talent. I asked them what kinds of talent they were talking about and they told me that, for example, a boy called Amir would make up cheers.

As it was obvious that I didn't understand what they were referring to, so I called out loudly, "Amir, sing some cheers for us! Show me what you can do." He started cheering for the faculty, calling out things like "The Faculty of PE is the best!" and all of the students repeated the cheers after him.

Younes joined us in the front and we walked to the accompaniment of Amir and his cheers for an hour, and this was how we entered the city of Assiut. It was a big scene. Younes and I were walking together, fairly quickly, with around fifty boys walking behind us cheering, "Captain Younes is our role model! Captain Younes is our role model!" In the middle they cheered for me once or twice, but reluctantly.

We reached Assiut University by five, and they had to leave, so they started taking pictures with us. At this point, we were standing by the Nile and the view was amazing. One of the students came over to take a selfie with me, and he asked to have it with the Nile in the background. I refused, because I didn't know him and the request was quite impertinent, then I found him putting his arm around my shoulder. With a sharp look, I told him that this was unacceptable and that I refused to take a photo with him, and I left.

That day Osama stayed at the hotel almost all day. He came over when we were just celebrating walking over half the distance to join the celebration. As he saw the students of Assiut University approaching me for photos, Osama gave me one of his looks and stayed by my side. So I wondered what he would have done if he were here and saw this guy's impertinent request!

"I got stressed," I told Younes, after everyone had left.

"By what?" he asked.

"Because of these gatherings, being surrounded by strangers all the time," I replied.

"Oh, I enjoyed it," he said.

"I did as well, but when it lasted too long I started getting stressed."

After few moments of silence, I continued, "What has been your best moment so far?"

"Moments like these, with the young people, feeling their enthusiasm."

"And what about your worst moment?"

"Ummm, I am not sure. The first week was a bit stressful for me—the talk with Ahmed and the press release issues . . ."

"Yeah."

"What about you?" he asked.

"I enjoy it the most when I'm with kids—walking with them, their cheers, and their smiles."

While walking, I heard Younes stumbling over something. He was a few steps behind me and I looked back to see that he had stumbled over tree pots made of rocks on the sidewalk.

"Are you alright?" I asked.

"Yes, but this is the second time today that this has happened. There seems to be negative energy around."

"But you can overcome it by your positivity, no?"

"Yes, I can," he replied. But I knew he was right.

When the students were walking with us, Maher, the stalker, had been trying to take a leading role and wanted to boss the other students around but I had to keep telling him to just walk in the line with the others. After they left he disappeared for a while but then suddenly reappeared and continued to walk with us.

He walked with Younes most of the remaining two hours of the day, and Mohsen came over to walk with me. The police accompanied us all the time, but they weren't imposing or restrictive to the same degree as the others had been. We reached the sign that read "Goodbye from Assiut," and it was already dark. The crossing of new borders had become less and less exciting. I looked behind and didn't see Younes, but found Maher approaching me.

I asked Mohsen where Younes was and Maher replied that he must have gone to pee, he had been walking with Younes in the back and left him in the dark, so I didn't trust him!

Ignoring Maher, I once again asked Mohsen, "Do you know where Younes is?"

Mohsen gave the same answer as Maher and I stopped to wait for Younes.

The police came over to my side and from the car told me, "You can continue your walk, and he will follow."

"No, I'll wait for him."

"Don't worry—we're with you," they insisted.

"I'm worried about him, not me," I said in my mind. "No, I'll wait," I told them. "It's better that we walk together."

At this point I found Younes emerging from the bushes. I waited for him to come over, and we continued the walk.

We talked a bit about Maher. That day, I had done a few different, surreptitious tricks, so as not to walk beside Maher, but I found Younes walking and chatting with him every now and then.

"I'm amazed at your capacity for tolerance," I told him.

Younes smiled and took two steps forward to walk by Maher's side. I thought that maybe I should try to be more tolerant as well, so I went over to them.

Younes observed to Maher, "But it seems that you're getting tired."

"No I'm not," Maher answered, "but you're walking too slowly, which is tiring me."

"Well, we don't have anything we need to do besides this walking, so we can take our time, and we need to make sure not to get injured," Younes replied.

"But I prefer to walk faster."

I couldn't help but interject, "If I were you, I would have walked ahead of us."

"What shall I do?" Maher asked, as if clueless.

"Life is choices," I answered simply.

This exchange was enough to convince me that I didn't need to be tolerant with someone I found so rude, and I strongly preferred not to walk with him the last few kilometers that day.

When we finished our day's walk we rode back in the car without telling him when we planned to start our walk the next day. If he didn't like walking with us, why was he?

That day, we covered 45 km and we were aiming to walk for 50 km the following day, so that we could take a rest the day after. I was in deep need of a rest day. I needed to wake up without an alarm, to keep eating all day, to act like a tourist and visit some attractions and to wear something other than sportswear.

I wasn't feeling well on this day and I preferred not to have dinner with the others. I asked Mohamed to take me to the accommodation if it was on our way, and it was. I had leftovers from two days before to eat, and I wasn't that hungry anyway. I went to bed thinking about the next day, the last day before our break! I was excited at the prospect of a rest, and also about the new record we were due to make—walking 50 km in one day. We were going to change hotels again by the end of the next day and it all contributed to making me feel full of hope and anticipation of a new start.

Day 15
ASSIUT
Assiut
45km – 8h 59m

Asyut

Day 16

IN THE MORNING, at five am we were packing. We had been supposed to meet at five but we were fifteen minutes late and for once we needed to give Mohamed a morning wake-up call.

At five-fifteen I was the first in the lobby. I gave Mohamed a call and he told me that he would be right there. Then I heard the sound of the elevator. I looked to my left and found Younes getting out of the elevator, for some reason looking taller than usual! He must have lost some weight. He went to the restaurant and got a takeaway cup of tea, then Mohsen and Mohamed both arrived and we hit the road at 5:35.

We had to walk in a straight line along the narrow road, Younes and I, with Mohsen sleeping in the car. The first two hours of the day passed so slowly. There was nothing on the road—no villages, no passersby—only fast cars came in both directions.

I asked myself why I was doing this. And the truth is, I was numb and couldn't find a direct answer. In the film *Forrest Gump*, when Forrest starts running, the question he is always asked is why he started, but when he stops the question becomes why he stopped. I started remembering all the people we met on the road, remembered the days of pain and how I became stronger and discovered new limits in myself. I remembered crossing the bridge over the Nile on foot, witnessing the sunset with its shades of blue and orange and the birds flying peacefully over it. I remembered the first day, and my feeling of pride raising the Egyptian flag. I reminded myself that, without this experience, I would have never known my country as I knew it then. I also remembered that Osama was not walking with us anymore. And I remembered Ahmed and the lesson I had learned—to know someone, you need to see how they treat others. And, despite the pains, I found I was starting to look forward to what was coming next: there were more people to meet, more events that would happen and I knew I hadn't reached my breaking point yet.

After two hours, we reached a village, Sukkarah, and I was like a fish finally in the water; life started to go on. We stopped for a short break. I took off my heavy jacket and put the light one around my shoulders. Younes had a bite to eat and in eight minutes we resumed our walk. The road became a bit wider and there was enough space for us to walk side by side.

Suddenly I found him whispering to me, "It might be better if you wrap the jacket around your waist." I didn't understand what he was saying at first, but after a moment I understood and did as he said with no questions.

Over the last couple of days, sometimes I would wrap the jacket around my waist but for efficiency purposes—to put it on and take it off depending on the temperature—but since he had specifically advised me to do it now, it meant that perhaps someone was watching or perhaps after I had gained more muscles my pants are getting tighter! I didn't know if the whole situation was an example of sexism, but the truth is that in every culture there are certain norms that it is better to conform with—at least to make life easier.

"Maher is texting me," Younes told me.

"Don't reply," I answered quickly.

Maher repeatedly texted Younes and called Mimo to find out where our spot for starting our walk would be. Younes didn't respond and Mimo didn't pick up because he knew that Maher wasn't welcomed with our group.

Out of the blue we found Osama coming over, telling us with only a trace of irony, "Surprise!" And we were more than surprised, we were horrified; yes were surprised with Osama's presence; he had followed us with the support car but he was sitting in it all the time and we were horrified to find Maher with him. It turned out that because Maher had known where we had stopped the day before and where we were heading, so he took a microbus in this direction.

Younes and I were momentarily speechless, and we continued walking without stopping to say hello. This could have been considered disrespectful by him and it is not common in our culture in general; in Egypt we have an open house culture but the truth is we felt we were being stalked, which is scary. When Maher first showed up, it turned out that he had Googled each of the team members and checked our social accounts and because he had the attitude of Mr. know-it-all and was challenging us all the time we weren't inclined to welcome him anymore, yet he showed up the next day uninvited.

Osama knew how frustrated we were with Maher. So we did something mean without intending it: I started to walk in front of Osama and Maher, Younes came to walk by my side and then Osama did the same. The three of us became like a walking wall, with Maher walking behind us. We stayed like that for many kilometers, but then Osama slowed down a bit and he continued walking with Maher.

After a while we stopped for lunch, took the cars, and went to search for a place to eat. We left without telling him anything. Nevertheless, we found him following us in the police car that was there for our security. That was totally bold and cold of him.

We found a cafeteria and were settling in when we found Maher coming in. He sat down at the end of our table, silent. Osama started teasing him, saying that we were preparing for another challenge and we might need someone as strong as him to join the team. Maher got excited and started talking about his achievements, telling us that he was a swimmer and a runner and licensed as a lifeguard. He didn't understand that Osama was making fun of him. Osama continued teasing Maher and started talking about him. "So I was talking with Maher, and I found out that today, he woke up by coincidence, put on his clothes by coincidence, left his house by coincidence, took a microbus by coincidence, and found us by coincidence." He was making fun of what Maher had said when he was asked how he found us; that he found us by coincidence.

Then Maher went over to address Mohamed, our driver, outside. Mohamed came in and told us nervously, "This guy is asking to speak to my manager. He isn't happy that we left without him. I told him that no one except the team is allowed in my car, and now he wants to talk with my manager." It wasn't only Younes and I who weren't at ease with Maher, but the support team as well. He was demanding that they provide him with food and beverages along the walk, as if it was his right.

The event management company represents the manager in this situation, and only Ramzy was there then. I looked at him and he was silent. So I looked at all the other team members, and everyone was silent, when I looked at Younes he was focused on his laptop and I know that he respects authority and Ramzy was the one who was supposed to answer then I looked at Osama; he was looking down. Where did all his chivalry go?

I looked at Maher and he looked back at me smiling. I had to say something. At that point I didn't care about authority, or that we didn't want to give anyone ammunition to talk negatively about us. I only cared about Mohamed's rights and felt the obligation to stop Maher, and since no one spoke up, I did.

"I don't understand what made you think that you have the right to ride in our car and go everywhere with us?"

"I was just asking," he replied.

"Just asking means that you think that you might have the right to make these demands," I replied. "Look, you came to walk with us, and when you come at lunch they provide food for you, but the car is for the team. When the Red Cross team comes to join us, or the students, they come in their own car. They don't expect to use the team's resources without previous arrangements. Furthermore, you can't talk to any member of the team in this way."

We left the cafeteria and departed without Maher. He came after us in the support car. He asked me for a photo but I said no, as politely as I could. I didn't trust him and was wondering what would the caption that he may write with the photo if I agreed to take one with him. Maybe something like, "I walked with them for two days and I was faster than them," or, "I walked with them for two days and they depended on me in everything."

We started the walk without inviting him to join us, but he did anyway. I could see Younes's attitude towards him starting to change.

"I will call Mimo," he told me. "He should make Maher leave, as he's responsible for the young people joining our walks, and yesterday Mimo was the one who brought him in the morning."

I knew he was right. Not only did we find Maher rude, but his constant presence was a bit creepy. Besides encroaching on my personal space and being an annoying presence during our walks to us and the support team, he also had looks that I found really scary, often staring in a way that I found very weird.

"I agree with you," I told Younes, but I didn't feel good. Younes called Mimo, then we heard Maher talking on his phone for almost fifteen minutes, then he left without saying anything to us.

Younes came over to my side. "We had to do that," he told me.

"I know," I replied.

He took a few steps back and I was left thinking, but he came back shortly. "You shouldn't feel bad about it."

"It isn't the best thing."

"No it isn't, but we had to be tough."

"I'm not upset about what we did; I'm just sad about him."

"And why so?"

"I sympathize with him. He seemed not to realize what he was doing."

"But what can be done about that?"

"I don't know . . . maybe we could have told him? I don't know. I'm just sad for him—I guess he isn't stable."

"If we didn't do that, he may have come again tomorrow and the day after. All the time he wanted to show that he was better than us, and he kept encroaching on our space. I was going to fall several times."

"I know," I said.

I had been mad at everyone when no one spoke out earlier to defend Mohamed. Was Younes reacting late to the issue? Or was he waiting for the right time and thinking simultaneously of the right move? My response had been spontaneous and, I believed, necessary for the situation but Younes took action to take care of the problem and its effects on us. Moreover, he wanted to make sure that I was okay and he assured me that we weren't wrong or rude in what we had done. Anyway, I was glad that he was there.

After a few moments of silence Younes continued. "He has an inferiority complex. Do you know what that is?"

"Yeah," I replied, but then wanted to ask him, "But are we still talking about Maher?"

Ahmed was still on a break and showed up only in lunch times. Today he and Osama were there and Osama told me to what extent he and Ahmed were proud of me. I replied as I believed: that it was all because of God's blessings. I wasn't physically stronger than Ahmed or

Osama, but I had fortunately been blessed, having received no serious injuries.

That day, we had walked 30 km before lunch and we had only 20 km to do afterwards. Yes, only 20 km! By that time, 20 km felt like easy business. Before six pm we were done.

"This was a good day—we achieved a lot in a very good time," Younes told me.

"Yes," I replied, smiling, then paused for a moment. "But Nadia will be joining us starting tomorrow and I'm afraid she will slow us down."

"Don't worry. We have a system and anyone that comes needs to abide by it," Younes replied.

We covered 50 km that day. It was a true accomplishment, especially given that it was done in nine hours of walking time. Younes and I found that we had been faster over the past two days. We started at the agreed time, took our rests as planned, and walked at a fast pace. We meant to walk for as long as we could so we could take a rest day and now we finally could. We had eight days of our challenge left and a rest day would make us stressed for the other seven days, but it was doable.

We got into the car, feeling incredibly tired and headed to Minya, where we had been told we would stay at a nice hotel. We needed that—I needed a comfortable bed! Reaching the city of Minya, I was sitting in the front seat and despite being dark, it was clear that the Nile corniche was wide and beautiful. The traffic lights were big and seemed new, the main street was nicely paved. I looked at all of this contentedly from the window, thinking that I would have the chance to see it freely in the morning, but five minutes before we reached the hotel something happened.

Younes told me, "I have bad news for you."

I had noticed that he had been engaged in something all the time we were in the car—an hour and forty minutes. It turns out he had been checking the routes and the distance remaining to Cairo.

"We won't be able to take a rest day," Younes said, definitively.

I was looking ahead, and didn't react.

"But you can do it," he hastened to assure me.

He didn't understand the reason for my silence, so I knew he was trying to make me feel better about it.

"It's okay," I finally replied.

But I wasn't okay. I couldn't really explain my reason for being annoyed. It wasn't the shock, and it wasn't that I thought I wouldn't be able to continue. It was much deeper but I didn't have the energy to explain or even understand the reason for being upset. I was drained. We reached the hotel, and while we were taking our luggage from the truck of the car, Younes looked at me for reassurance.

"You can do it," he told me.

"I know," I replied.

We took our luggage and entered the main door of the hotel, which was huge. We went down a few steps, the main restaurant was on our right and then there were other steps down to the lobby. We entered the lobby and signed the check-in paper, then we went to another restaurant by the Nile in the same hotel.

Nadia had arrived and joined us at dinner, bringing a new spirit to the group. She was fresh and she wanted to have fun, which was something we missed in the group. Sitting at an Italian restaurant by the Nile, Younes was at the head of the table, I was on his right, Osama on his left, Nadia beside Osama, Mohsen by my side, then Ahmed, then the rest of the support team on the other side of the table. We all had pizzas and pastas except Nadia, who ordered a salad. The food took a long time to be served and we were extremely hungry and tired.

Nadia had already started posting on Instagram about the challenge and creating stories. "Oh, your mum just liked my post," she told Younes excitedly. "Does she follow me?"

"Yes, I guess," Younes replied.

"Oh, I'll tag her in a story . . . oh, I just realized we have the same name!"

"Of course you're pissed off now," Osama told Younes.

"No, my mum can do whatever she wants. She's my best friend, by the way," he replied.

The pizza arrived, but the salad didn't. We started on our pizzas and Nadia started to get upset and prepared to leave because she had asked for her food several times, but just before leaving it was eventually served. I only had two pieces of pizza and gave the rest to those who were still hungry and headed to my room.

We had almost completed two thirds of the distance to the finish point and I was exhausted—more mentally than physically. There was something wrong with me that I couldn't exhaust the effort to figure it out and my presence had become an essential part of the challenge now. The days of asking myself whether I would be able to do the entire walk or not were over; now they were depending on Younes and me for the success of the challenge. So the question had become how I would manage to do the entire walk, not if I would manage to do it. And I was worried about the changes in the dynamics of the team—in the past sixteen days, there had been many changes. The next day Nadia was going to join us, and Osama, now feeling better, had decided to get back on the road as well. I went to bed hoping that these changes would be for the best.

Day 16
ASSIUT
Assiut, Dairut
49km – 9h 27m

Part 3

The day before we had stopped 9 km before entering the governorate of Minya on foot, we had almost 330 km left to reach the finish line, and we still had four governorates left to walk out of nine. We were not having a rest day but Osama was getting better and decided to hit the road again, and Nadia too was going to walk the last eight days with us. And during these days, I had my first clash—or clashes—with Younes.

Part 3
MINYA – BENI SUEF – GIZA – CAIRO

Day 17

AT FOUR-THIRTY AM we all got wake up calls from the hotel. I had slept okay the night before. I was tired of packing and unpacking, so I just took out my pajamas and what I was going to wear the next day and left it at that. During the first two days, when we were in Aswan, we had changed our clothes before going to dinner, but now by this time, we barely had the strength to eat our dinner itself. We were staying at the Grand Aton Hotel, and for me the room was just the right size: there was just enough space to move around and it had a big bed with a comfortable mattress. It was overlooking the Nile, but I couldn't take advantage of that view because we moved before sunrise.

We met in the lobby at 5:25 am. I left my bags in the room and handed in my keys in the lobby for the event management team to check us out, because we were staying at that hotel for only one night.

We were in the car at 5:50, and I found Mohsen approaching us at a rapid pace before we set off. He passed Ahmed's watch to Younes and told him to give it to me. The day before, Ahmed had texted me to say he was proud of me and that he would do anything to help me continue. He wanted to give me his watch, which was a sports one with a heart rate sensor, of a kind I didn't have. I took the watch from Younes, thought for a moment, and then wrapped it around the car's door armrest and did up the strap.

In the same message Ahmed had also told me that he had brought new shoes for Osama. He said that probably the main reason for his injury was him wearing tight shoes. He wears size 49 and the largest size we could find in the market was 48. After Osama's injury, Ahmed had been asking friends in Cairo to see if anyone could find size 49 shoes in any shop, and one was successful and sent the shoes to him. So now Osama could walk more comfortably.

It took one hour and forty-five minutes to drive to the starting point, where we had a decision to make. Up to that point, we had always taken the longer routes around the villages instead of going through them, but the difference had only ever been 500 meters. But passing through Dairout, the largest city in Assiut, would save us 1.5 km, so we decided to take the shorter route. As we entered the village, it was early in the morning and not that busy. We walked along a two-way street with a wide canal, Ibrahimiya canal, on our right, and houses and shops on our left.

For the next hour we all walked together, Nadia making a story on Instagram. We passed a historic dam, Dairout Barrage. It was built over a hundred and forty years ago and is one of the oldest hydraulic projects in Egypt, serving agricultural land in Middle Egypt. Besides the economic benefits it brings, it is an architectural beauty, and it is the point where the canal divides into two branches, with one of those branches eventually ending up in Fayoum, a city in Middle Egypt. It was designed by Egyptian engineers, and many poets of that period wrote about it. I walked a bit ahead of everyone to take a few photos, then we gathered again.

When we had passed through Dairout, Nadia needed to use the toilet. Being new, she didn't know the system yet, so we stopped at the nearest gas station and I asked where the toilet was. As she made her own way there, Younes asked me if I wanted to pee as well but I didn't. I understood that he wanted us to go at the same time, just like my mum used to do when my family was on a road trip. But by this point I was used to peeing in the lunch breaks. Nadia came out and we started walking again. It was a sunny day and I asked her if she had a hat, but she didn't. I knew she would need one. After a few minutes she stopped to take off her jacket, then after another few minutes she stopped to take a photo. I decided not to stop with them that last time, as I needed to continue walking. The day before, we had walked 50 km per day to be able to finish the distance in time and I knew that we would need to walk another 50 km for one of the coming days. I was physically and mentally stressed, so I couldn't stop every now and then and risk losing momentum.

I was walking on my own and wondering what was happening in the back. I knew they were having more fun and I was a bit jealous, but I still couldn't slow down. I started thinking about what had been bothering me since the day before. There were a lot of incidents that had happened over the past few days, and I had really needed the day of rest because my mind resolves issues in my sleep. Sleeping for only six hours at the most was just about enough for my body to heal itself, but it certainly wasn't enough for my mind to sort out and absorb all the events that had taken place. I suddenly found that I had completed the first 10 km myself. I wanted to wait for the others but I wasn't sure how far behind they were. I had found myself ahead of the team many times before but I had always maintained the connection by keeping them within sight. I hadn't been walking that quickly, so they must have been stopping a lot, I thought. When I had finished 15 km I knew that I should call Younes.

"Hello?"

"Hello."

"Where are you?"

"A little behind you."

"I've walked 15 km. Should I wait for you?"

"Whatever you like."

"How many kilometers have you walked so far?"

"Thirteen."

"Umm . . . I'll carry on walking by myself till the lunch break then, or should I wait?"

"Whatever you like."

"I'll carry on then."

And so I did. I'd calculated that if they were taking eleven minutes to walk 1 km that I would have to wait for twenty-two minutes for them to catch up with me, which I felt was too long. I wasn't happy to be on my own, and I was upset without knowing the reason, then after five minutes Younes called.

"The police want us to stay together."

"Why?"

"So they can secure us."

"Umm . . . can you pretend that I'm not with you?"

"What?"

"As if you are only three?"

"How come? We need to stay together."

"Okay, I'll wait."

I knew that I didn't make sense to him but all I was thinking was that I didn't want to wait for twenty minutes, which meant that I would lose twenty minutes of daylight. I sat down on the sidewalk. Mohamed was behind me in the car, and he told me to continue walking and ignore the police, but I couldn't because I had told Younes that I would wait for them. Mohsen came over and sat by my side, which made it worse because then I couldn't even shed few tears privately if I wanted to. After another five minutes, the police arrived.

"Finally we found you."

"Welcome," I said.

"You should all stay together, for your own safety."

"There's nothing to be afraid of," is what I wanted to say in retaliation, but I didn't have the energy to argue, so I just kept sitting in silence.

After another seven minutes Younes, Nadia, and Osama arrived.

"We were only 1 km behind you," Younes said.

"My device said that I've walked 15 km," I replied.

"That's not right, but anyway we had to stop because there was a chick emergency," he said with half a smile at the corner of his lips, which he wasn't good at hiding.

"Okay," I answered, but internally I was fuming. *Chicks. Chicks!*

We had another 10 km to walk before lunch time. I quickly moved a bit ahead again, but this time by less than a hundred meters. Younes came over and asked me what I wanted for lunch.

"Anything whatsoever," I replied rudely.

"Do you want sandwiches or meals? I'll have a chicken Super Crunchy, but you can have whatever you want."

"Sandwiches are good. I can have shish tawook," I said.

I continued walking at my pace and he slowed down a bit, so we parted. I felt so bad that I wanted to cry just because of how I was talking to him, but I had something else bothering me that I had to figure out and resolve before I could apologise or make any effort to be conciliatory. I remembered Maher the stalker—but no, I wasn't bothered about him anymore. I remembered Momen wanting to force on me the idea that statues are haram, but I knew that this also wasn't what was bothering me. I remembered the police with the rifle, the accident, the men from the Red Cross invading my personal space but none of that was what was playing on my mind. Then I remembered the young girl and her shoes that got torn off, and I remembered Sohad and Safa.

Sohad was one of the girls from the Red Cross who had walked with us in Qena. She had told me about her life and about her dad, who was sick in the hospital. When we stopped for lunch, she had disappeared; we then heard that she left to go to her dad, as he had passed away.

Safa was also from the Red Cross and she walked with me in Sohag, the day after I walked with Sohad. She came because she wanted to understand what we were doing. She wasn't wearing sports shoes but she told me that the ones she was wearing were comfortable. She walked with me 20 km that day, having never imagined she could do such a thing. She told me about her life as well, completing her master's degree. She wanted to be a professor, and despite having an adventurous spirit she had had a very tough year. She wore a black skirt, black blouse, and black headscarf and it turned out that both of her parents had passed away in the same year. Her mum had died first, and a few months later her dad followed. I felt overcome with sorrow when I heard her story, but it wasn't my place to show it. I tried to give her a feeling of positivity and hope, but I suppose I didn't realize how it had affected me.

I thought of Safa and Sohad and I felt scared. I wanted to call my parents to check on them, but I also wanted to go apologize to Younes. I allowed a few tears to come down first, to release the tension, then I pulled myself together and slowed down until he was by my side. I raised my head a bit towards him, without looking at him, and said, "I'm sorry." I found my voice was breaking as I said, "I was just stressed out." I wanted to show that I was okay, so I smiled. "Now I'm back."

He looked at me and affirmed, "Yes, you're back now" with a smile, then patted me on the back and said, "Don't worry, and if you want to talk . . ."

Before he could finish, Nadia took two steps forward and came between us and said, "Yes, it's very stressful . . ." but I didn't hear the rest of her sentence because by then I had already moved two steps ahead—walking in silence with them, and not.

Little by little, I started loosening up. Then the food was almost with us, and we had the mission of finding a place to eat. We found a nice renovated cafeteria in Mallawi, a town in Minya. It had couches and tables next to the walls, and chairs and tables in the middle. We sat in the middle, waiting for the food. Nadia posted a story about the chicks on Instagram, and about how impressed she was by Osama's act of goodness. It turned out that they had found a box of chicks on the side of the road. All the ones on top were dead, but Nadia had wanted to see if there were others alive beneath them. She asked Mohamed if he had an empty box in the car. In the beginning he had said that there wasn't but she had insisted on searching for something. It turned out there was an empty box in the car.

"Osama was a hero," Nadia said. "He courageously started to search for live chicks amid the dead ones."

"Nadia, I told you not to post about it," Osama said, but Nadia refused to listen to him. Then she continued talking, saying that with all this going on Younes had wanted to continue walking because I was alone in the front. She said that, and looked at me and him.

The food arrived, we ate and I ordered French coffee and went to one of the hidden couches to lie down a bit and raise my legs. Osama sat on the ground and raised his legs on the wall. Younes raised his legs on one of the chairs, and Nadia was still fresh. The support team played backgammon at a separate table beside us.

At two-thirty we hit the road again. For the first forty minutes we all walked at the same pace, and then I started to walk a bit faster, at my own pace. At four-thirty I found Mohamed coming to me in the car and handing me his phone.

"We've found a nice location and we'll stop for a photo session with the videographer. If you'd like to join us, Mohamed will drive you over," Younes told me.

I thought for a second and then I told him, "Okay, I'm coming."

I stopped the tracker, pinned my location, and went back to them. They were standing beside a photogenic old house. I joined Younes, Nadia, and Osama in the shot, then we had a walk in the fields where they took more photos of us. After twenty minutes we were rushing to hit the road again because we didn't want to walk in the dark for long, especially since the police wanted to leave. Osama told me that Mohamed could take me back to the front to pick up from where I left off.

"It's okay, Osama, I can walk from here," I replied.

"But why? It's better that you go from where you stopped."

"I'm fine, Osama," I said.

"She can walk this extra kilometre," Younes told Osama.

We started the walk, but Osama rode in the car because his feet were hurting and he shouldn't walk on them for long or else his injury would worsen.

We walked the remaining 10 km together: Younes, Nadia, and I. The canal was very wide on our right and the fields were open on our left, with the sun vanishing from between the palm trees. The police officers were getting tired and upset, so Younes gave them dates and they were immediately better.

In the car, Younes sat in the back beside me and Nadia in the front seat. I remembered the watch and asked him to hand it to me. We reached the hotel at seven-forty, and thank God Hamdy had managed to book us another two nights in the same hotel. There is a prominent Christian festival that takes place at this time of year, so most of the hotels were fully booked and the city was teeming with people.

We were taking the stairs down, but I noticed that Younes was walking strangely. He was taking one step at a time, bending only one of his legs.

"What's wrong?" I asked him.

"Nothing, I just don't want to overuse my legs so as not to get injured," he replied.

I didn't really buy what he was saying, but he sounded okay. We went to the restaurant, then Ahmed came. I went to him and gave him the watch.

"Thanks, Ahmed, but I don't need it," I told him.

"But why?" he asked.

I was adamant. "I just don't."

Dinner was ready at eight. It was Egyptian pies, with all kinds of fillings: sausage, cheese, honey, cream, with butter, pastirma, and maybe more. There was enough to feed thirty people. I ate a few pieces of several pies and was ready to leave. Younes looked at me, so I went over to him.

"Tomorrow we move at six instead of five, okay?" he told me.

"Yeah sure," I replied.

I went to my room and remembered that we had told the police that we would leave at five. I messaged Younes and after five minutes he replied, "Handled, thank you for this."

It had been such a stressful day, but it had softened by the end. I was glad that things were sorted out for now, but I was still afraid about the coming days. Frankly, I didn't want to feel alone for the next seven days but I wasn't sure if there was anything I could do to improve the situation. Before I could over think everything, I fell asleep.

Day 17
ASSIUT - MINYA
Dairut, Mallawi
43km – 8h 42m

Day 18

OSAMA, NADIA, YOUNES, and I woke up early and met at six-thirty in the lobby before getting into the car. That day, we were going to enter Minya on foot. Days like this are exciting because we get to see the big cities—not only the villages on the road. What we had seen of Minya so far was awesome. The Nile was very blue and surrounded by green parks. On its east bank, there were villas and a pyramid-like building.

"Mohamed, what is that thing on the left?" I asked.

"The Nile!" he replied, with utmost confidence.

"No, Mohamed, I don't mean the Nile."

"Oh, then it's a park."

"No, Mohamed, I mean on the other side of the Nile."

"Oh, that! I don't know, let me ask." He opened the window and asked the police officer in the car securing us.

"The corniche," they replied.

We burst out laughing.

What I was asking about turned out to be a museum, the Aten Museum. It is focused on Egyptology and has been under construction for years, with its initial conception and design planned in 1998. Twenty years ago now!

We reached the starting point and began walking together. After two hours, the Minya Red Cross team arrived. They hadn't known about our arrival the day before. We liked having them with us; they added spirit and information to our walks. But they also came in their full uniform, including safety shoes, which made it hard for them to walk.

One of the team members had finished college; he had been at the faculty of PE. He was complaining that he wasn't going to be assigned to be a professor in college and that working as a PE teacher would not be financially rewarding. He wanted to open his own gym but he didn't have the financial means. I suggested that he try to find a partner who could finance him, but he told me that he didn't like to enter into partnerships. I was quite tough with him, telling him that starting a business requires agility and resourcefulness, and saying that if you are not open to trying different things, you will fail before you even start.

Then there was the man who thought that Egyptians were the smartest of all nationalities but that we didn't have chances or opportunities to succeed. His argument was that all the Egyptians who travelled abroad were geniuses. And my argument was that the smartest were the ones who made it abroad, and that many Egyptians travelled overseas but were not geniuses in their fields. He didn't want to abandon his way of thinking at first, and I understood that. I can see that it is easier when one thinks that the problem is outside of oneself. You can absolve yourself of responsibility. But then another man came over and backed me up. He too thought that it was not rewarding to work for the government, but he already had his own business—a sportswear shop in the city. There was also a physician in the team and he was very active; he was the one who gathered the team to join our walk once he had heard about the challenge. There were also three women who joined us. One of them stayed in the Red Cross car all the time, but three days later she became Hamdy's new employee, replacing Salma.

We passed banana trees, and my companions told me how the bananas were planted and transported. I remembered once when I had to pee and we had been walking through fields of banana trees on the way. The field was below the street level and the trees were three meters high in some cases, and clustered together, so while I was in the field no one could see me from the outside because the leaves would block the view. But when I was inside, if someone walked past he could easily see me. I tried to hide behind a tree, but it wasn't practical because banana tree fields are muddy. They need moist soil and humidity to grow, so my shoes were stuck in the mud. I came out of the fields looking funny without even accomplishing the mission.

We saw the gates that said, "Welcome to Minya" while I was walking with Younes and one of the Red Cross team. Again we played the game of guess the distance but this time to the gate. I guessed 2 kilometers our companion guessed one and Younes did not make a bet, I guess he doesn't like losing. I kept telling my companion that I would win but when we reached the gate we found out he was the most accurate.

The gate had a drawing of Nefertiti and the words "The bride of the Nile" written on them. Alexandria is considered to be the bride of the Mediterranean and Minya the bride of the Nile. Osama made fun of this and we stood together, laughing about it. I hadn't walked much with him for the past few days but I knew that he was having fun at the back with Mimo, eating sugarcane and lettuce directly from the field, or with Nadia as she rode on a donkey.

We went to the hotel, rested for half an hour, and then had our lunch there. Then we returned to where we had stopped, to continue our walk. We were going to walk through the city of Minya, but it wasn't as pleasant as I had thought it would be. The moment we entered the center of the city we felt anxious, as it was busy with cars, and polluted. The buildings were higher than anywhere in the south, and dotted around were complexes that seemed new but just looked like rectangular boxes. Many other houses were built in red blocks. It was getting sunny, and we found the heat combined with pollution and congestion a very irritating mix. We found a bridge to walk under which gave us shade for a while. Younes was walking a little behind with the police officer, who was of a very high rank. Nadia was walking quickly, ahead of us, listening to music with headphones.

That day we walked 43 km and finished at seven pm. We were at the hotel at seven-thirty. Once again, Younes went down the stairs strangely and I asked him again if he was okay. He told me that everything was better if he walked that way. I still didn't buy it, but when I watched him walk during the day, he looked fine. We went to eat in McDonalds after putting our bags in our rooms, and to our surprise our main sponsor came in to see us. After greeting him, I asked about the closing ceremony, whether it would be at three or four pm.

"Ehem, it will start at eleven am," he replied.

"What? That can't be."

"We don't have an option. The minister will be there at eleven and so you also have to be there at eleven."

These four or five hours would translate into 20 or 25 km. We had only six days left and we had just added 25 km to the distance we had to cover in our time period.

I was feeling exhausted from all the surprises, but at the same time I was becoming numb. I found myself thinking it was okay, we only needed to walk more kilometers every day. But at least the good news was they had bought caps for all of us.

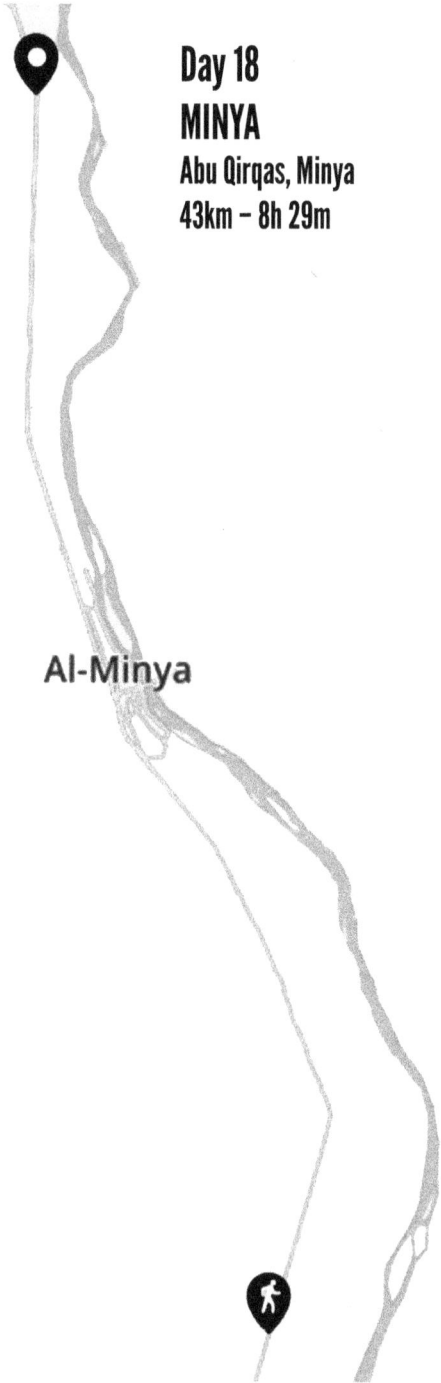

Day 18
MINYA
Abu Qirqas, Minya
43km – 8h 29m

Al-Minya

Day 19

AND SO THE tough days were back. We decided that we would not count the last day as a chance to be productive, because many students from different universities would be joining our walk, so we knew that we wouldn't be able to walk more than 15 km on the last day. So we had five walking days left and almost 250 km to cover. We would have to walk 47 km per day.

Osama wasn't feeling well, so Nadia, Younes, and I started moving from the hotel at six-fifteen. The day was extremely foggy we couldn't even see the car just ahead of us. We thought that the weather would clear up quickly but it didn't. Mohamed drove slowly until we reached our starting point. Getting out of the car, we could barely see anything. We walked closely together, Nadia, Younes, and I. Mimo and Mohsen followed us in the support car. To be honest, I find it beautiful when everything is covered in white, but it was a bit cold. Still, after an hour, it cleared up. We stopped for a few minutes to take off our jackets and refresh ourselves, then we continued our walk. But then Nadia stopped again to get something from the car. Younes wanted me to wait but I frowned and continued.

The canal was on our right with trees offering us shade and the birds were flying over the Nile, but still I was stressed. I wasn't sure what to do. I knew that stopping with the others every now and then wasn't the answer. I knew that I was adding tension to the situation by not being as flexible as I could have been, but I wasn't sure why I was the only one expected to compromise. In the past, each one of us had walked at our own pace and then we had gathered together in the breaks. Why was it different now? And why were they sticking to Nadia? I don't mind being a follower but to whom is of paramount importance to me. And this is one of my problems in corporate jobs—I just can't follow a manager just because of their title. If a person wants my respect and loyalty, he should earn it.

I knew that what I was doing was causing Younes stress, and I didn't want that, but I couldn't seem to stop myself. Should I say something, I wondered. But if the others didn't have a problem with the new system, then what could I say? I was like the black duck. Still, I thought, Younes had told me that we had a system and whomever would join us would abide by it. What had happened?

Another two hours passed and I found Younes by my side.

"We have to stick together," he told me.

"But it's safe and I don't see a reason why we have to walk in a capsule."

"I'm not saying that we walk in a capsule, but two days ago I had to call you to ask you to wait for us."

I paused for a moment. "Yeah, and I called you and asked you if I should wait and you told me I should do what suited me."

"Yes, but if I'd been you I would have waited without asking."

I didn't have anything to say to that.

Younes continued, "And the police can't secure us when we're far apart."

"For the past two weeks, that wasn't a problem."

"But here it's different."

"But we can't stop every time someone wants to pee or take off their jacket or just take something from the car."

"We're a team and we should be together . . . it's not a race."

These two phrases created a storm inside my head. What? A team! Not a race?! I knew these weren't Younes's words. What's going on here? I thought.

With all of that going on inside I replied, "No—it isn't a race, but I was always walking ahead. From our first week." He looked at me but I didn't understand his look. I hoped that it was the realization that whatever had been said to him wasn't right—or at least, not all of it.

"Yeah! But still we need to be together. Not necessarily in a capsule, but not far away."

"Okay," I replied, and slowed down a bit.

After a few moments, "Are you okay?" Younes asked, looking back at me.

"No, I'm not," I answered quickly. But this moment and this question made all the difference. No matter what the rest of the conversation might have led to, this question was enough. I don't know for what, but it was.

"Why not?" Younes asked.

"I'm afraid that the remaining days will be shitty."

We found the support car stopping in front of us and Osama getting out of it, but continued walking fast and furious, as if we hadn't seen him.

"It isn't pleasant if we have to stop every time anyone stops, and we didn't do that before. In the past anyone who stopped, rushed to catch up with the rest of us," I continued.

"But not all of us can do that now. And Nadia is here for social media, so she needs to stop to do some posts and so on."

"Exactly—so we're not a team. A team needs to have the same objectives and we have different ones."

"I'll tell her to post less while we're walking. I've already agreed with her on that."

"Okay, that's good." I didn't really think that was an option but if it was it would make a big difference. If he had told me that from the beginning maybe we wouldn't have had to go through all that, I thought.

"And we have two options," Younes continued. "Either we stop when everyone stops or we all stop together every 10 km for five minutes."

"I prefer if we all stop every 10 km."

"I also prefer that."

I was so relieved by this conversation. But not only that—for the past eighteen days I had been afraid to form an opinion about Younes. The behavior I had seen from someone I had known for years made me suspicious about everyone. But in that moment, I knew that he was someone I could trust.

After 23 km, we stopped for lunch. Younes, Nadia, and Osama were standing together so I went to them and apologized to Osama for walking past him earlier. We got into the cars and headed to a restaurant to eat. The place was called Nutella Coffee Lounge and it was in Beni Mazar town, still in Minya. It had two levels, and when we went upstairs it was huge, with many seats. We were the only guests in the place. I went to sit beside Nadia, and Osama sat in front of us with Younes beside him. The support team was on the table just beside us.

Osama wanted a crepe with Nutella, but he was suspicious. "Excuse me," he said to the waiter. "I wanted to know, is the chocolate in the crepes Nutella or something else?"

"I'll ask the chef," the waiter replied.

Even though the place was called Nutella Coffee Lounge, that didn't seem to be enough to guarantee that they would use Nutella in their ingredients! Nadia ordered seafood soup and a salad. The rest of us waited for the food we had ordered beforehand. We were now used to getting food from somewhere and eating in the nearest place we could find. The soup was too heavy for Nadia and she couldn't drink it, but the salad was okay. She decided she would only eat salads and fruit from now on. After eating, I lay for a while on the couch with my jacket over my waist and hips to cover up a bit. Then we had our drinks and were back on the road.

We had 24 km left to cover that day and I was already feeling heavy. We all started together, as we always do, but this time I could walk at my own pace without feeling guilty. After a few kilometers, a distance started to form between me and the others, though I was walking slower than usual. But I wasn't alone this time; I had members of the Red Cross team accompanying me. We passed many small villages. There was nothing special about them except that the road was narrow and the sidewalk wasn't always there, so we had to keep stepping up and down to walk on the sidewalk whenever possible. I stopped after 10 km as agreed with Younes, and he was proud of me. He didn't say anything, but he gave me a thank you look.

After another 15 km I found Younes beside me.

"How did you catch up?" I asked.

"I walked a bit faster," he replied. "I didn't ride in a car, of course."

I was astonished because he had been at least 500 meters behind me.

"Where is Nadia?" I asked.

"It's okay, she isn't on her own," he replied.

The night had fallen and, as you know by now, I don't like walking in the dark. The road was a two-way road and there was no space for Younes and me to walk side by side, so I invited him to walk in front of me.

"But where is Nadia now? It's getting dark and it's better to walk together," I told him.

"Don't worry—she can ride the car whenever she wants. She doesn't have to walk the whole distance. She's here for social media," Younes replied. That was weird, but not worrying.

We had 5 km left when we found Nadia getting out of the car to walk with us along with Ramzy. Nadia and Younes walked in the front, and Ramzy and I just behind them. We talked about Samy, who was better and had started college after his break. Then Ramzy started telling jokes. He had so many jokes and I had none.

After covering 2 km, I had a sudden strong pain in the lower calf of my right leg. I thought that the pain would go as it always does. The usual thing was to get sudden pain somewhere, then find that it fades away after a kilometer or less. But this time it was just too strong. I didn't know what to do—should I ask them to stop, or continue the last 3 km? If I carried on walking, it might get worse, but we couldn't stop because we needed to reach Cairo on time. Should I tell them? No, I will just continue and see, I decided.

"Younes, how many kilometers left?" I asked.

"Two," he replied.

"Why are they walking quickly?" I asked myself, but they weren't and I knew it. Ramzy was still by my side talking, but I just wanted to scream.

"Younes, now how many km left?"

"One and a half."

Nooooooo, I wanted to say out loud. I tried to walk quickly as I always did, to finish as soon as possible, but I couldn't.

Fifteen minutes later we stopped. I went to sit in the car as soon as I could and closed my eyes. We started moving. I took off my shoes and started rotating my ankle and massaging my calf carefully. It took us an hour and a half to reach the hotel. Just before we arrived there, I decided to tell them what was going on. This wasn't the right time for my ego to win. Younes and Nadia were in the car, with Younes in the front seat and Nadia beside me.

"Guys, I have a very bad pain between my calf and ankle."

"That's the Achilles tendon," Nadia said.

"No, I think it's just the lower calf muscle . . . or I hope so," I replied. The truth is, I was super scared. We got out of the car, took our things from the truck, and I started walking down the stairs on one side, just like Younes had been doing.

I went downstairs, looking for Mohsen. Osama and Ahmed helped me look until we found him. I was standing and the three of them surrounded me, waiting to see what might be wrong.

"Mohsen, I just want you to tell me if this is a muscle pain or the Achilles tendon. I don't want it to be the Achilles. I hope it isn't." Apparently I was panicking.

Mohsen was too calm for my liking. "Okay, I'll wash my hands and see you."

"Okay, I'll put my stuff in my room and come to you." I went to his room and found him, Ahmed and Osama waiting for me. Without many questions I lifted the leg of my trousers, and asked him to check my legs. He kept pushing in different places, then he told me that it was just muscle strain.

"So it isn't the Achilles tendon?" I asked excitedly.

"Mohsen can give you a massage," Osama said, worriedly.

"No, I'll be fine. I don't mind muscle strain . . . I'll wake up fine."

We went to the Italian restaurant at the hotel. We were all there except Nadia, who needed to rest and hadn't been able to eat anything since the seafood soup. Younes received a message and told us that we would each need to report the distance we had walked. Ahmed was startled and asked why this was necessary, but he didn't wait for an answer. I told Younes that I had walked the same distance as he had so far. And Osama surmised that someone probably needed the information for the certificates.

We were quieter than most days. I was in pain and the guys might have been thinking about the certificates. Younes was sitting by my side and he looked at me and told me that I could rotate my ankle both ways to feel better. I told him that Mohsen had told me that it was the muscle, so I wasn't worried anymore. The food was served and I ate two slices of pizza and left to go to sleep and allow the healing process to start.

Day 19
MINYA
Beni Mazar
47km – 9h 54m

Day 20

I WAS UP at four-thirty am and we had agreed to walk 50 km that day. What was I thinking? I put my feet on the floor to stand up, pushed myself up, took two steps forward to try my legs, and they worked! It was a new day, and the one before consisted only of memories. I had returned to my room and taken a warm shower, immersing my calf for several minutes to relax the muscles. I went to bed and massaged my leg a bit. The soles of my feet were very painful as well, red and inflamed. So I had had to sleep with my feet raised above me.

We met at five in the lobby, Younes and I, as no one else was joining. Nadia wasn't feeling well and neither was Osama, and we had started to forget that Ahmed should even be walking as well. We started at Maghaghah, a city in Minya that one of the Red Cross team had told me she lived in. This girl was a fighter. We had talked about friendship. She told me that she was one of a group of four close friends and they didn't let anyone else in their circle. It had taken them such a long time to find each other and they didn't want anyone to disturb the stability of their group. This girl had a heart condition. She didn't think that she would live long but she had decided to pretend that she was okay and live her life to the fullest. She didn't like submitting to weakness, saying that it was like a living death for her. And this group of best friends were always there for her during her hardest times, cheering her up, helping her study, and taking her out.

We crossed Maghaghah to the tunes of Avicci, with the canal on our right and agricultural fields on our left.

"Would you like to listen to something different?" I asked Younes.

"Sure."

"Try, *Begin Again*."

"Which song?"

"Just let the album play."

Beginning with a gentle guitar ballad, We enjoyed the beautiful addition of upbeat piano tones of Lost Stars as we walked. Keira Knightly begins singing softly, "Please don't see just a girl caught up in dreams and fantasies."

"Did you see the movie *Begin Again*?" I asked Younes.

"Nope."

"It's my favorite—it's a must see."

"Yeah?"

"Yeah, *Begin Again* is a movie that might fall under drama/romance, but it isn't a love story. It's a life story. It's a story about taking opportunities, being spontaneous, and living life to the full. It's about people we meet who disappoint us because of their greediness and others who are inspirational even if we only meet them briefly; their presence helps us be at our best. It's a story about life choices and coincidences, and how when we leave the things that are wrong for us we find what's right for us."

As the music picked up on tempo, I got caught pausing to listen to Keira's beautiful voice singing, "Searching for meaning, but are we all lost stars trying to light up the dark."

I continued, "In the last scene Keira's character is shown riding a bicycle. We don't know to where, but the important thing is that she is paddling. It reminds me of my favorite quote from Einstein: 'Life is like riding a bicycle. To keep your balance you must keep moving.'"

Keira continued that the way we see ourselves is crucial, it may turn into realty and we shouldn't dare to let our best memories bring us sadness, everything is possible; she has seen enemies turn into lovers and we can always have new starts.

"What's your favourite movie?" I asked Younes.

"*The Usual Suspects*."

"What's that about?"

"It's a mystery. Five con artists meet to plan a major robbery and in the end only two survive. One of the survivors gets interrogated and we hear his version of what happened."

"Is that's all? You won't tell me more?"

"No, you have to watch it."

"Ummm . . . do you like reading? I bet you do."

"Yeah, I do."

"What type of books?"

"Nowadays I like reading inspiring true stories. Ahhh my watch!" Younes exclaimed suddenly, looking at it.

"What about it?"

"The battery's low and the charger is in my bag with the event management team. If it dies, today's record won't be saved and we will lose track of the distance. I'll call Hamdy." So then fifteen minutes later, Hamdy arrived with Younes's bag and the charger. It had been a close call, but now all was good.

Charging our appliances was one of things that weighed us down a little. I only had my mobile phone but if I used it to listen to music and German stories all day, take photos, check the Internet, track the distance we walked, and pinpoint the locations we stopped at (because that was my responsibility), then I needed to charge it twice a day. I had a power bank but it was small and I only had one charger. So at the end of every day I charged my phone while sleeping, then in the morning I would give my power bank to Mohamed to charge it in the car. When my phone battery had only twenty percent remaining I would charge it with the power bank, then give it back to Mohamed to recharge it. And so on. Younes had his mobile, speakers, watch, and power bank which he had to charge every night.

At ten am we found the Red Cross car approaching as we were crossing the border from Minya to Beni Suef. At first we thought this would be the team from Beni Suef, but it turned out to be the Minya Red Cross team. The physician had been afraid that the Beni Suef team would not arrive on time and that we would be walking without an emergency team. I was so touched by how thoughtful this was of him and grateful that the rest of the team were so responsive to him as well. We all walked together but in pairs, in a line. They walked with us for two hours beyond their territory, then the new team arrived. We bade the Minya team farewell and found that the new team was a bit sleepy. They had been summoned at short notice and apparently it was too early for them.

We had already walked 20 km so Younes knew we would have to stop for a break soon. He was walking with police officers who told him that we would find a place to sit in Al Fashn. I was looking at the map and I found that we were taking the longer of two possible routes.

"Younes, should we continue or go back and walk through the city?"

"Oh no, better to go through the city to look for the cafeteria the officer told me about."

We walked a little way back, then entered the city. Al Fashn had a different ambiance, with old houses. It turned out to be a historic city that had been around since the time of the pharaohs. It reportedly has the biggest families in Beni Suef, as well as some sectarian strife between Muslims and Christians. It is a busy and bustling place, with tuk-tuks were everywhere. We were walking along, searching for the cafeteria, but it turned out to be at the end of the city, a 3 km walk away.

I looked inside the cafeteria from the street and found it too sunny, without enough shade. "Younes, it will be very hot in there."

"I guess there's another one over there."

"Yeah, that has plenty of shade."

"It doesn't have the same facilities as the other one, but you check them both and choose whichever you prefer."

We took the car and I checked both and decided on the shaded one. It was covered with khayameya cloth, the ground was sandy and it had wooden benches and tables, and plastic chairs. It wasn't the worst place we had been to.

Shortly afterwards we found Osama, Nadia, and Ahmed arriving in a taxi. The taxi driver was driving crazily and Nadia was extremely angry that the event management team had put her in a taxi, which she took as an insult. But the other cars were filled with our luggage, because that day we were going to stay at a new hotel in Beni Suef. She was also angry because they weren't catering to her nutrition needs. We were eating chicken almost every day and she prefers healthy vegetarian food. I tried to calm her down a bit but she really needed to vent.

Nadia, Osama, Ahmed, Younes, Mohsen, and I sat at the same table, the Red Cross team at another and the support team at a third. Whenever Nadia was around, there was action. She kept posting funny stories on Instagram and informative ones about our walk. She and Osama were becoming a great duo. They were hilarious together. They told jokes and read the comments that fans were making on Nadia's stories. One of the fans liked Osama's calves. That became one of our jokes for the rest of the trip.

The three of us started walking together—Nadia and I, with Younes a little way behind us.

"What's your plan for after the walk?" Nadia asked me.

The walk had come to me by chance and I wanted to build on it, but I didn't know how. After a short talk, she told me that I should keep following up with Younes on the issue, but Younes had already given me his input, which was simply that I should try. Nadia then started texting on her phone and slowed down, so I continued walking. When I had told Younes that I didn't know how to build on what we were doing when I returned home, he had told me to write about it. I didn't like the answer; that wasn't what I was looking for from him. Writing about it was already on my mind. I had written short stories about previous adventures and we definitely had a story here. But I wanted his advice on how to build on this from a sports point of view. He had only one thing to tell me: try.

The walks weren't as much fun as before. In the beginning, we met people in the street, talked with them, walked with young kids and we were experiencing everything for the first time, fresh. But as we continued north we looked more like the locals. We were closer to Cairo and we weren't foreigners to them, in the way we felt in the south. The traditions were less conservative but people were less welcoming as well. We had already walked past the most beautiful locations by the Nile and what was especially unfortunate was that we were starting to see more pollution in the air and in the canals. The water level in the canals was lower here than in the south and also there were many fewer birds.

After two hours I stopped to wait for Nadia and Younes in the car with Mohamed, eating a protein bar and drinking some water. The protein bars were among the main components in our nutrition. A protein bar was a healthy snack and provided us with the protein needed to rebuild our muscles. They were sponsored by an Egyptian company, Advanced Sports Nutrition (ASN). Five minutes after Younes and Nadia arrived we stopped for another five minutes so they could take their break. I had some water and we all continued for the last 10 km, to complete our 50 km together.

Nadia said, "Guys, you are beasts." I too had never imagined that I could do that.

By six-thirty, we had finished our walk, which was great as we hadn't had to walk far in the dark, but it was because we had started really early. We got into the cars and headed to our new hotel in Beni Suef the city. We had already entered the governorate of Beni Suef early that morning, meaning that we had only Giza left, then we would arrive in Cairo.

The hotel was an hour away, by the borders of the city. It was a health resort with a pool and a health club. When we first entered, we saw a table tennis table. I took one of the rackets and Osama the other and we started playing. We were awful; we were running after the ball more than we were playing the game. Then Hamdy came and took the racket off Osama in a rude way and he and I started playing. He plays well. Then Younes came over, and he looked at us playing much as a child looks at cotton candy. I gave him the racket and went up to my room.

The room was basic, which was okay. I had a shower, changed, and went down for dinner. We had made the order before I had gone up to my room. We waited at the reception and they told us the meal would be ready in thirty minutes. We got frustrated because we had made the order an hour ago. Nadia got annoyed and yelled at them but it didn't change anything. We went to the restaurant and waited there, until after an hour the food started to be served. In this hour, Osama started playing with Hamdy a flip the bottle game. This was a challenge to see who could flip the water bottle in the air for it to land on its base without falling.

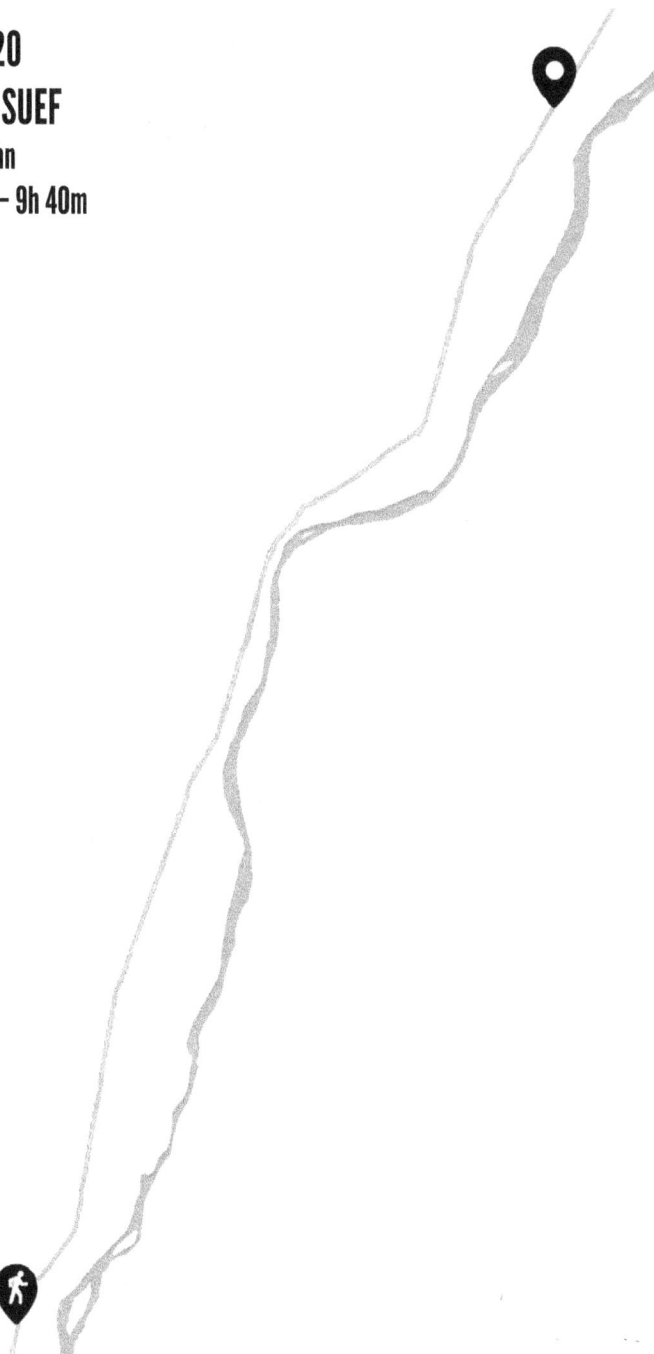

Day 20
BENI SUEF
El Fashn
50km – 9h 40m

Day 21

AT SIX AM we were ready to move, Younes, Mohsen, and I. The police objected because in their records we should be two cars moving, not one. After a lot of discussion, Hamdy came down and they agreed that we could move. The police car was in front of us but they were driving at a speed of 60 km/hr. Mohamed didn't have the patience for this, so he bypassed them and drove at 100 km/hr and the police started chasing us, or so it seemed. Mohamed usually drove quickly and whenever I sat beside him, I told him that I didn't want to wake up in the Nile. I mainly used the driving time to sleep.

But on this day, I wasn't asleep. Whenever we reached a new place I would keep watching from the window, and it was beautiful that day. The sun was rising and we were going mainly downhill, with the green fields ahead of us filled with palm trees. The police car suddenly came ahead of us and out of the blue we saw a shredded crow scattered in the air like confetti but more dramatic. It turned out that because they were driving too fast to catch up they weren't able to maneuver when they saw the crow that was flying too low and hit it.

We reached our starting point and Younes woke up. He had had his eyes closed for the entire ride. We got ready and started walking. To be honest, the start was weird. We felt no enthusiasm and didn't even have our three, two, one to start. We just started walking as if it were an obligation.

After an hour of walking silently, the Red Cross team joined us. There were more of them than there had been the previous day. We were due to have an event that day at Beni Suef University and there were students joining us, so they wanted to be ready for any emergency. There was a woman that started walking with me, and apparently she had had instructions that I was her responsibility and she took it too seriously. It is scary how we sometimes put more value into things than it's worth; maybe we need to feel that we are indispensible?

When we entered the gates of Beni Suef the city, Mohamed disappeared and it started to get busy. The streets were one way, with tall buildings on both sides and many shops. We had to cross the street and the woman with me wanted to hold my hand. I was annoyed. I don't like to be accompanied as if I am a child and I definitely don't like to be treated as though I am incapable of crossing the street on my own. I asked her to leave my hands alone, and we started a ridiculous Tom and Jerry chase—where of course I was Jerry.

In the city, there was a Carrefour and we walked down the one way road in the opposite direction to the cars. Mohamed suddenly appeared with falafel sandwiches and offered me and Younes one after the other; it was a delight. Mohamed was following us and at the end of the road we found a policeman who stopped and reprimanded him for driving in the wrong direction. He tried to argue with him and showed him the permits for the walking competition, but that didn't give him the right to break the law so the officer withdrew his driving license. I think on some level, we had all thought that we were above the law because we were accompanied by the police.

After passing through the city, we went to Beni Suef University for the event. The media was there to cover our challenge and we were all welcomed warmly by everyone, especially me. All the women at the university were hugging me, expressing their pride that a woman could walk that distance. I had met a couple of them at the opening in Aswan, and they started commenting that I had lost weight and that they were very proud of me. I had never expected such celebration, and was overwhelmed. They took photos with me, as if I were a celebrity. We then started a short walk with the PE students, going to a youth center. We were blocking the streets because there were dozens of us walking: the students, the Red Cross team, and all our team, including Ahmed.

At the youth center they had prepared a show for us, and we stayed for ten minutes but then Younes called me over because we had to continue our walk. Only the two of us left to return to the starting point and the rest of the team stayed.

There was something weird between us. We were walking together but not together, as if our magnetic fields were repelling. This was annoying me. We had walked quietly together for hours on many other occasions, but this time it felt different. I was reluctant but decided to ask him; taking a deep breath, I looked back at him.

"I need to ask you something . . . are you angry with me?"

"What? No, not at all. Why would you think so?"

"I wasn't sure but I've been feeling this for a while."

"How long?"

"Ummm . . . two days." During the walk each day felt like two to three days, depending on the incidents that took place.

"What? Two days . . . I'm not angry at all, but there are many things in my head."

"I'm glad it's not personal."

He started to tell me about some of his issues, and then we found a bus full of students and the Red Cross team coming over, and our team as well. I walked with the girls at the front, while Younes, Osama, and Nadia came just after us with the boys.

At one-thirty, we went for lunch. We took the car and drove 500 meters to the nearest coffee shop, which was in the street between two car repair shops. It was very noisy but we sat there anyway. A reporter came over while we were having our drinks and she started shooting us as if we were on a reality TV show. She focused on small details: Younes sipping his tea, Osama taking his last bite of food, me with knee bent and my feet on the wooden bench, Nadia's facial expressions as she talked about how she was touched by the celebrations, and Ahmed posing with a straight back and a smile on his face.

Then she interviewed Younes and Ahmed, and she decided that that was enough. She had come with Ahmed and I didn't know what they had agreed on while they were on the way. I gave Ahmed a look that he understood.

"I think you should interview her as well to represent women," he told the reporter.

"Okay then," she replied.

We had a nice interview and then we went to continue our walk. She shot us while we put on our shoes and prepared our trackers, and she shot a small part of the walk. We were all walking together, the five of us, happily. After 10 km, Ahmed got tired and got into the car.

I started walking with members of the Red Cross team. They were treating me like a minister who was surveying the country's newest projects, showing and telling me about all the landmarks of the governorate.

"And here are the Sods silos. There are six silos and they have the capacity to store twenty-five percent of the wheat produced in Beni Suef," one of the team told me.

"Beni Suef has the Nile and the sea," another one said.

"What? How?" I replied.

It has the Nile river and the Yussef sea."

"What is the Yussef sea?" I asked.

"It's a lake," he replied.

"Oh, yeah."

After a while, they continued. "And on the other side of the Nile, you can see the biggest natural gas power plant in the region."

I was acting as if I was knowledgeable about this subject, asking questions and nodding my head. I then found Mohamed approaching me in the car and handing me my jacket.

"Younes sends you this," he said.

I took the jacket and put it around my waist without hesitation. I wanted to look back at him but I didn't.

Then I had found one of the Red Cross members limping. It turned out that he had a massive car accident months ago and he had had many surgeries in his leg. He was walking with us since the day before and he wasn't supposed to walk such distances.

"You have to rest!" I told him.

"I can continue."

"But why risk harming yourself?"

"Well, my mother also didn't want me to come today. She told me that one day was enough. But I told her that if a woman can do it then I can."

"So you are here just to prove that I am not stronger than you?"

Another member told me that the day before he told his colleagues that there was a woman who walked from Aswan till Beni Suef and they didn't believe him. He came again to prove to them that I was walking the whole distance and not riding the car in the middle.

When the night came, the Red Cross team left and the police officers started getting tired and bored. One of them kept walking beside Younes while he was on his motorcycle, and every ten minutes he asked if we hadn't walked far enough that day. I then walked with him for a while, and Nadia kept making fun of it, telling me that he liked me. But the guy was married with two kids.

There was a sound coming from the bushes on the side of the street. At first I thought it was dogs and then we saw a black dog coming out of the bushes, at night I didn't dare to bark with the dogs, I was afraid they would attack me. When the dog left, the sound in the bushes continues, it turned out it was full with rats . . . eww. I tried to keep away from the bushes as much as I can yet far from the road.

When we had only 5 km left, Ahmed got out of the car to walk with us. I was in the front and I saw a sign that said it was 100 km to Cairo, the middle of the city. I took a photo of it and posted it on Instagram and Facebook.

Ahmed walked over to me. "Is that true?" he asked.

According to Younes's calculations we had 130 km until we reached finish line. I didn't give Ahmed a clear answer and continued walking. Younes had always doubted the signs on the road, he was certain that his calculations were more accurate.

At eight-thirty pm we had completed 45 km, and that was enough for the day. We headed back to the hotel, but this time we weren't very far away. We went straight to the restaurant beside the hotel, where we had pre-ordered our food. Nadia was beside me and kept telling me that I had to eat well, but like every day I just couldn't.

She then told us about her fight to become an athlete. She had had a heart problem since birth and the doctors hadn't expected her to survive. Her parents were therefore incredibly protective and she wasn't allowed to participate in PE lessons at school. But then at college she had started hiking and triathlon. Although her mother was worried, Nadia insisted on continuing. So finally she went from not being able to participate in PE at school to hiking mountains.

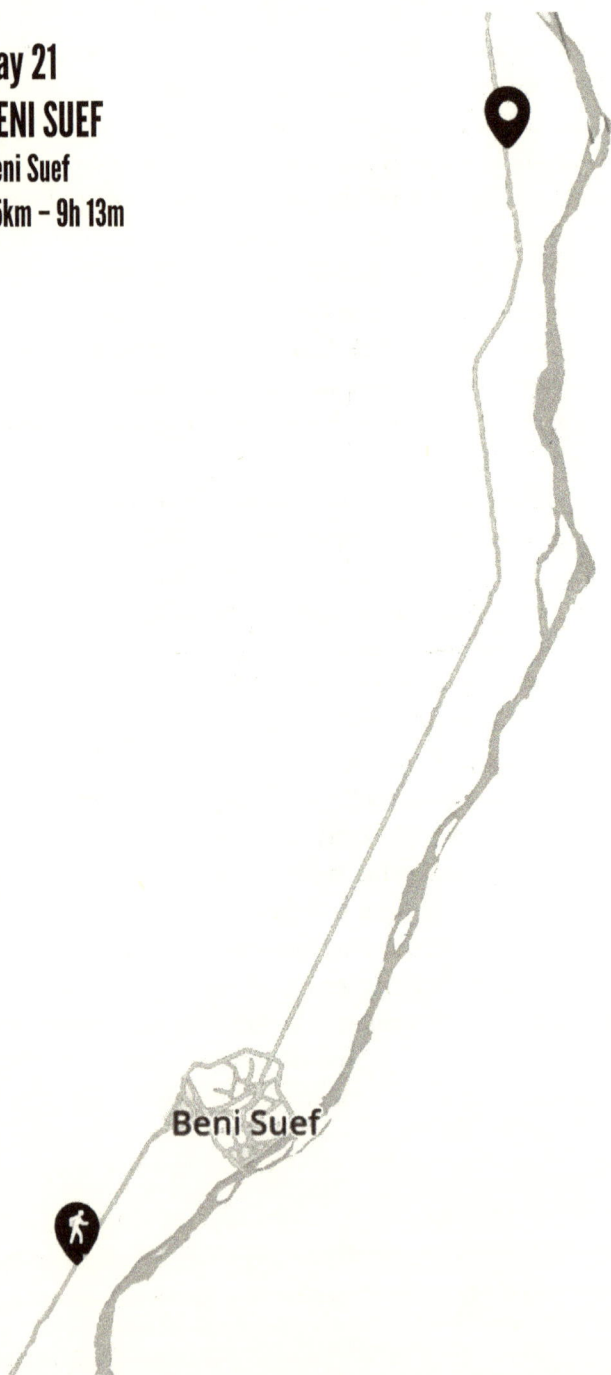

Day 21
BENI SUEF
Beni Suef
45km – 9h 13m

Beni Suef

Day 22

WE HAD MADE it to the twenty-second day! Wow! I had a conversation with Younes on one of the days.

He told me, "You will feel the value of what you are doing when we finish."

And I told him that I enjoyed things along the way, not simply the accomplishments and the accolades at the end. We had been through a lot and had many surprises, most of which were negative, but . . . there is always a but and this time it is positive, now we were about to have some happy news.

I was the first in the lobby with my luggage, because we were checking out that day.

I found Hamdy approaching me and asking, "Would you please check the distance from here to Mazghuna, in the governorate of Giza?"

"Forty-five km," I told him.

"And from there to Cairo?"

"Forty-one km," I replied.

"So we are not even 125 km away from the finish." He smiled.

"You'll need to double check that with Younes."

Younes came down and Hamdy went over to tell him the news. We went to the car and Younes started checking the route, before confirming that we had only 86 km to reach our finish point.

We went over to the starting point, and said the words "three, two, one and start." I felt high as a kite with the news.

"Younes, let's tell the rest of the team the news."

"You tell them."

"No, we should tell them together."

I started recording a voice note. "So guys we have news for you."

I put my mobile closer to Younes so he could tell them the news but he shook his head.

"Okay," I continued. "Guess how many kilometers are left to reach the finish line, and the one who guesses right will get a gift from us."

The team started guessing. Nadia said 50 km, then Mimo said 150 km, then Osama said between 55 and 65 km, then Nadia said 96 km according to the street sign she had seen the day before. Then I broke the news. There was excitement in the group—especially from Osama, who was proud of us.

Mohsen was walking with me and Younes, and we saw a level of happiness that we hadn't seen for a long time now. Mohsen was a hero; he had been with me and Younes all the time in case of any emergency. He had walked half the distance with us, and he was in the car the other half of the time. He must have been bored because Younes and I hadn't asked much of him. But he was dedicated, and every day he woke up early in the morning to start the day with us.

One of the police officers came to walk with me. This was the second day he was with us and he had a question for me.

"Are you married?" he asked.

"No."

"And don't you want to get married? Sorry for asking."

"It's okay, but why do you ask?"

"Because with your level of energy, it's hard to find a husband and settle."

"I would like to get married, but not to settle. I've traveled around a lot and studied abroad, and now I've walked Egypt. I don't want a husband to just lean on."

"You want someone so you can grow together."

"Exactly! To experience life and learn together."

"So how do you spend your days?" I asked him, after a brief pause.

"I have a small piece of land. I wake up early in the morning to work on it, then I go to work and work on it again when I return, and that's all."

"Do you have kids?"

"Yes, I have two kids."

"Do you want to have more?"

"Look, no one with two kids can afford to have more nowadays. That's more than enough."

There seemed to be a huge difference in the mentality of employees and tribesmen. Employees and small farmers depend on their salary at the end of month or the minimal income of a small plot of land, so that they can live. They worry about affording a living for their wives and children. On the other hand tribesmen live with an attitude of abundance, whereby the more populous the tribe the stronger it is. They want their business, land, weapons, or opium to stay within the family. They don't want to hire strangers, so it is important to them to have many children. And they are forbidden from marrying outside of the tribe, so as to save the land from being divided into pieces, benefitting men who are not part of their tribe. It isn't only women who are without the freedom of choice in tribes; men also can't choose who to marry freely or when to marry. Everything is decided for him. A tribe is like a company; every member in it works or lives for its sake.

We walked quietly for a while, and then I found a dead animal by the canal. The canal looked as though it was in the midst of a drought. And the only thing filling it was garbage.

"What is that?" I asked, gesturing to the dead animal.

"There's a gang that comes from the mountains at night, takes the donkeys' skin, and leaves them to die."

I was stunned.

"I had a donkey and one day we woke up to find it skinned. What happens then is that the owners of the animals throw the beasts away beside the canal, and other animals eat them."

The mountains surrounding the Nile look beautiful from the outside, but they are perfect spots for smugglers and gangs to hide in. They are hard to reach, and contain many hidden places.

At eight-fifteen we reached the borders between the governorates of Beni Suef and Giza. In terms of learnings, I considered us finished at this point. Giza is not a foreign governorate for Caireans. Yes, I haven't been everywhere in my city, but fundamentally the citizens of Giza and Cairo are alike. Or no—in Giza and in Cairo, no one is like anyone else, so maybe that's what we have in common. But at least both are industrial and commercial cities more than they are agricultural ones, and both are very busy all the time.

Younes and I took a photo with the police officers of Beni Suef and Giza at the border, as well as a picture with Mohsen and one with

Mohamed, and we continued. These are the most precious pictures to my heart, as Mohsen and Mohamed were heroes with us on the road.

At ten-thirty the rest of the team joined us, so there were five of us on the road and the support team. Nadia, Younes, Osama, and I were walking together and Ahmed was ahead of us. We were all relaxed now. We listened to music and talked about general topics.

Then suddenly Nadia became very animated and said, "I don't understand men and I never will."

"Just treat them as if they know everything, and they will do whatever you want," I told her.

Younes smiled and Osama wasn't really following the conversation.

"But women aren't so rational themselves," Younes said. Then he added, "They are super important of course. I wouldn't be here if not for women, but sometimes they are a bit crazy."

Then out of the blue, my mobile phone flew out of my hands and fell far away.

"And this proves my point," he said. It was hilarious.

I wanted to pee, so I started to walk faster, looking for a gas station or a mosque but there were none. The police were following me like my shadow, but in the car this time. I found a cafeteria on the other side of the road but knew that if I crossed the street suddenly it would alert the police.

"Sir, I'll go to the toilet in the cafeteria over there," I told the officer in the car just behind me. He started getting out of the car. "No, I can go by myself," I told him.

"I will go with you wherever you go," he said firmly.

He got out of the car and crossed the street with me. I found Mohamed getting out of the car as well to accompany me.

Younes was 50 meters away, so I called him, "Report, report. I am going to the toilet."

"Where?"

"In the cafeteria on the left. The police and Mohamed are with me."

We went inside. I was going to ask the waiter where I could find the bathroom but the officer didn't let me ask, and simply told me, "Straight ahead on the left."

I headed there, entered the bathroom, then found them standing by the door and closing it from the outside. I am nobody! I thought. I peed, washed my hands, and knocked on the door for them to open it for me. I went outside and found Younes waiting for me and the rest of the team.

"It is time for our five minute break," Younes told me.

We continued our walk but we were getting tired and hungry. It was a sunny day and we were starting to relax so we were feeling the tiredness in our bodies. There was a restaurant on our way that we were going to walk to. As always when I am tired, I walk quickly to try to reduce the time period. Osama was also tired and he was ahead of me. Younes, Nadia, and Ahmed were a little bit behind.

I reached the restaurant, which was called El Shelenk, and was in El Ayyat, an area in Giza. It turned out that its name had a story. The food was authentic Egyptian cuisine and the restaurant was all in ceramic with wooden tables and chairs. I sat inside at first and when the rest arrived, everyone came inside but Nadia. The restaurant serves mainly meat and she not only didn't eat meat but didn't even like the smell, so she decided to sit outside. Osama sat with her and I went to join them. Osama told us the story of the name.

"I asked the waiters what it meant. They told me that it comes from the word 'hook' because when we grill a chicken we hook its legs. 'Hook' in Arabic is pronounced 'shankel' and for an unknown reason this became 'shelenk.' So the name meant hooking."

When the food was served, I went over to Younes and told him that we were eating outside but he and Ahmed joined us after lunch. Nadia was angry that the event management company hadn't taken her nutrition needs into account but the service at the restaurant was awesome. The waiters didn't want her to be angry so they got her some salad and white cheese, and she was happy and grateful to them.. We had our tea outside, and then the owner of the restaurant arrived and insisted on taking a picture with us. I don't know if he knew who we were or not, but we did look important with the police cars accompanying us.

At three we continued our walk. I started texting my friends to encourage them to come join us for the last day. It was a big day for us and for the challenge. Most of my friends had work that day and couldn't join us, but two are business owners and they promised that they would do their best to come. They were athletes themselves and so excited about our walk. These were two of the guys I had texted a thank you message to before the challenge started. This seemed so long ago at this point.

"Guys, I don't know what to tell my parents," I told Nadia and Younes.

"They don't know that you're walking?" Younes asked.

"Not really. I didn't know that I would walk the whole distance, and when I found myself doing it I didn't want them to worry about me getting tired or injured."

"You have to tell them," Nadia told me. "They need to attend the closing ceremony and they'll be so proud of you."

I called my mum and I asked her if she knew that I was walking the whole distance. It turned out that she already knew because . . . she just knew. I told her that they were invited to the closing ceremony and she was eager to attend.

I was getting really tired by five and I wanted to pass the time.

"Younes, tell me a story."

"What kind of story?"

"Any story. Tell me an adventurous story! You must have many."

"There's nothing in my mind now."

"Oh come on! All right—tell me a suspense story."

"Ummm, it's difficult. I can't think when I have to think; it needs to be spontaneous."

"I understand."

Ramzy came to walk with us. He is a talker, and he discussed many different things before returning to the car.

"Younes, have you thought of a story?" I asked.

"I wasn't even thinking about it," he replied.

"Okay, I'll tell you one. I was in Verona, in Italy, and it was one of my last days there. Like most cities, it looks small on the map. I decided to take my chance and walk to the train station. It was a 2.5 km walk and I had a 25 kg bag and a 5 kg backpack. It was a hot day, so when I reached the station I was tired and in dire need of cooling down. I had the best iced coffee you could imagine and headed to the platform I was supposed to take the train from.

"Luckily I was early. So I sat for a while drinking my iced coffee and then I had the feeling I was in the wrong place. I went downstairs to look at the screen with the trips to and from Verona, and I kept looking at it for a long time. Something was wrong but I couldn't figure out what. Suddenly I found a man who works at the station standing beside me. I told him that I wanted to go to Munich and he pointed to the other screen. I had been looking in the wrong place! I know this was stupidity on my part, but after fourteen days traveling around, I had lost my focus. When I looked at the right screen it made so much sense, and so I headed to the right track.

"I got onto the train and sat in my reserved seat. I was traveling from Verona to Leipzig, Germany. It was a long trip, especially because I was a low budget traveler, so I took a cheap night train where I had to change four times before reaching my final destination. So I made a wish. I wished that the train would be running late so I would arrive in Munich late, and then the train company would compensate me by putting me in a hotel for one night in Munich, so then I could take the first train in the morning directly to Leipzig.

"In the train I found a young woman approaching me. She asked me if I spoke Arabic so I said yes. She wanted to check that she was on the right train and she looked very confused and worried. She asked if the seat beside me was taken and I responded that it wasn't, so she sat next to me. She asked me several times if I was sure that the seat wasn't reserved and each time I reassured her. I asked her where she was from. Reluctantly, she answered that she was from Egypt. I told her that I had thought she was from Sudan because she looked more Sudanese, and she replied that she was from the south of Egypt, in an unfriendly way.

"I paused for a while then asked her what she was doing in Germany. She replied curtly, 'My brothers are there.' So I decided not to ask any more questions. She kept calling her 'brothers' every fifteen minutes or so to tell them her current location and to make sure they would pick her up. Then she started getting annoyed and I heard her telling the person she was calling to tell someone else to pick her up. Then she asked me if I had a passport! I replied that I had. I didn't think that this was something even to question in the first place. Who can travel without a passport? I wanted to ask her if she had one but I decided not to. Sometimes when I don't want to hear a specific answer I just avoid asking the question. Then she asked me if I could buy her a ticket from Munich to Cologne when we got off the train. I asked her why she couldn't buy the ticket herself and she answered that it was because she doesn't speak German. I really wondered (and still do) how she was able to travel from Egypt to Italy and then to Germany without knowing any Italian, German, or English. Anyway, I answered that I couldn't, because I had a train to catch from Munich and I was afraid that I didn't have enough time to buy a ticket for her, but I did write down her destination and told her to give the paper to someone in the ticket office and that they would guide her. She didn't seem happy about this and was very worried. And to be honest, I was too. I felt unsafe. I had so many questions and the possibility that she didn't have a passport scared me. She could have been a thief; she could have been anything.

"After we had crossed the border into Germany, and we were some 50 km away from Munich, the train stopped. At first we didn't know what was going on. After ten minutes, an announcement was made that there was an investigation taking place and the train would stop for another fifteen minutes. I told the girl beside me what was happening so she could tell whomever was picking her up that we would be late and I went to sit somewhere else."

"She was there illegally?" Younes asked.

I nodded.

"So then what happened?"

"After another fifteen minutes there was another announcement that the police needed fifteen minutes more. So we stopped for around forty-five minutes in total. In this time, I saw people getting off the train accompanied by the police. I saw men, families with kids, women, all from Africa or the Middle East. During those forty-five minutes, I had mixed feelings. I was sad for these people, running away from the countries where they belong into the unknown, to a country where they can't even speak the language! And I was also asking myself how the other people in the train would think of us and what will they think of me. Was I a suspect too?

"I looked back to see the girl and she was gone. Then the police came. They knocked on the bathroom door . . . once, twice, then finally she opened it. They asked her for her passport, and of course she didn't have one. They asked her for her luggage, and she didn't have anything! So they took her and then they approached me and politely asked for my passport. I gave it to them and told them that I could show them the residence permit as well, but they told me that all was ok and they gave me the passport and left. Of course they didn't check any Western-looking person which makes sense.

"I felt humiliated and I knew that I had missed my connecting train. At that point I had stopped wishing for them to let me stay overnight and take the first train in the morning directly to my final destination. I only wished to be treated fairly.

"When we arrived in Munich, I started carrying my luggage out of the train when suddenly I felt the bag was much lighter. I looked behind me and found a German man helping me with the bag. I felt relieved. It was good to be reminded that people don't treat others badly if they are not afraid of them. I went to the ticket office as did most of the other people on the train because we had missed our connecting trains. And guess what? They offered me a free night's stay at a four star hotel and a direct train the next morning to Leipzig, my final destination."

"Ohh, that's a good one," Younes said.

But there was something that I didn't tell him. I had doubts. I had stayed fourteen days in Italy and had a great time. People had been good with me and everything was nice. I had had fun and I had had fights as well, but fundamentally I felt at home, though it was with a different culture and religion. So I found myself questioning, if I was right, or they were, or if we all were right in our own way.

When I was on the train and I had had that wish, I'd never thought that it would come true. But with everything that happened and the treatment I got from everyone, I got my answer.

We were supposed to walk 45 km that day but after we had finished 42, I was really tired and we had the opportunity to stop. I asked the others if we could and they didn't mind. We went for dinner in Cairo, where we would be staying for the next two days or until the end of the challenge. We ate at Mince, a burger restaurant in Zamalek and Nadia became angry again and returned to the hotel without eating. We had our dinner and then went to the hotel to check in. I almost fell asleep on the chair in the lobby, waiting for the team to finish all the procedures of checking us in. Hamdy made sure that Younes and I were the first to get our rooms. We were late, and the next day we were going to meet at five-thirty am.

Day 22
GIZA
Al Ayyat
43km – 9h 33m

Day 23

WE HAD 42 KM left to cover over the last two days. On Day 23 we walked 33 km and we left the last 9 km for the finale, stopping at a convenient meeting point for the students and friends who were joining the last day of our walk. In fairy tales, usually everything gets resolved at the end, but in real life there is no end. Every moment can be an end to the previous moment and a beginning to the next moment. Every day was new, and at any given moment we couldn't predict what would happen next.

We moved from the hotel at five-fifty am and passed On the Run on the way. It is a cafeteria in a gas stations which serves good coffee. I had my first decent flat white since . . . since . . . it seemed like forever. It was nice being home.

At seven-forty we were at our starting point. We were all together: the five of us plus the support team. We were relaxed about the challenge, but the road itself was so stress inducing. The pollution was very high and the roads were wide, with many trucks. The only good thing was the music.

"Your music is getting better," I told Younes.

"It's the same playlist," he answered.

"There are more things on it."

"Yeah, one or two."

At almost the same moment Nadia told Younes, "Are we going to listen to the same playlist over and over again?" She then put her songs on instead.

As we were all walking together we were moving quickly, wanting to pass through the area, but because the sidewalk was not connected we had to go up and down a lot. Younes and Nadia talked about future plans and sports figures. I wasn't participating in the conversation but Younes always kept a space for me to walk beside them.

At some point, Nadia put on her headphones and started walking at a faster pace ahead of us. She wasn't focusing on the surroundings at all when a truck left a garage and nearly hit her. She stopped and screamed, and the driver braked just a few centimeters away from hitting her. Osama immediately pulled open the driver's door, grabbed the driver by his shirt, and started fighting with him. It reached the point where Osama was hanging from the window outside the truck when the police appeared, pulled Osama down, and forced the driver to come out, before withdrawing his license. We went over to Nadia, who was unharmed but panicking a little. She kept repeating that she had nearly died.

A little while later I was walking on my own when one of the team members came over and started walking with me. He told me that he had heard Nadia the previous day complaining to one of our colleagues about many things, including me. She thought that I was jealous of her, saying that I was avoiding her all the time and whenever she came to walk with me I would leave her and walk away. He told me this and then got into the car.

This stressed me out. Yes, I was jealous, but not of her. I was jealous on the first two days because the others were all together and I was on my own. I knew that Nadia didn't like me personally; she always asked Osama and Younes to sit with her or go with her or join her in whatever she did, and not me. But we were on good terms whenever we interacted. Moreover, she was encouraging and had shown care. This new information had left me with a heavy heart and whenever I feel stressed to that degree, I have to shed a few tears to feel better. So this is what I did and then I started to think more clearly. I wondered why that person had told me what he had heard. He shouldn't have, especially because he told me not to say anything to her about what he told me. I decided that I would ignore what I just heard, as if it had never happened.

We reached our end point for that day. By that time, we were in Giza city, which is in Greater Cairo. So technically we had reached Cairo. My happiness made me forget about any worries, and Osama and I danced in the street. Then I took a photo with Younes, celebrating our accomplishment.

It was two-forty pm and we had the rest of the day to eat and rest. So we just relaxed in Cairo, eating lunch in Maadi and dinner in Zamalek. Traveling in Cairo often means spending long hours in the traffic. Younes, Nadia, and I were in the back seat and Osama in the front, and we had some nice chats and laughs.

Day 23
GIZA
Dahshur
33km – 6h 28m

Giza

The Finale
GIZA – CAIRO
9 km – 1h 43m

THIS WAS THE first day that we didn't have to wake up before the birds. We went to have breakfast. Younes was sitting at a table for two with a new girl, while some of the support team were sitting at a table of four. I went to sit at a table of four next to Younes's.

Then Hamdy came and sat with me. While eating, he leaned towards me and told me, "We have a position for you at our company if you are interested." He said this with a confident smile.

I responded quickly, "Maybe we can talk about that at the end of the day."

I wasn't happy about his proposal. The timing wasn't appropriate, at least for me, but maybe he thought that he was giving me good news.

Then Osama came to join us at the table. Initially, he was going to sit beside Hamdy on the other side of the table, but I asked him to come beside me so as not to block the line of sight between me and Younes. This way, we would be all sitting together.

We left the hotel at seven-twenty, reached the starting point at seven thirty-five and waited for everyone who would be joining our walk till eight-thirty. Then we started. Students from three different universities had come—many of whom were women. There was TV coverage, and newspaper reporters. We did several interviews then we started the walk. Younes and I were in the front, leading the walk. He was wearing the Egyptian flag on his shoulders and we walked proudly, the rest of the team always around us.

One of my friends texted me that he wasn't able to join because of a work emergency and the other just didn't show up. In the middle of the walk Younes stopped suddenly with a wide smile. A young man approached him and they hugged. It turned out this was one of his best friends, who had come just to see him but had to leave again for work.

We continued our walk, with the Nile on our right and skyscrapers on our left. Sailing boats and standing boats dotted the river and to the other side there were many international hotels.

I found Ahmed approaching with his fiancée behind us. They had got engaged one week before the challenge, and she was so supportive. I met her once and we got along well. I walked with her for several minutes then I went back to the front with Younes. Nadia was walking with us but I noticed she always tried to keep a distance and not to come in front of me. I think she was afraid that I would think that she was stealing my thunder. I tried to leave some space for her to walk freely in the front but whenever she was ahead she slowed down to be behind us. Osama had five of his friends joining our walk who he introduced as his brothers, and I thought this was true.

We were on El Nile street in Giza, and then we needed to cross one of the channels of the Nile, so we crossed over El Galaa Bridge. This was our second time to cross the Nile, and while it was brief it was a great feeling. The bridge was 160 meters but all its light columns had Egyptian flags waving in the wind. By crossing the bridge we arrived in Zamalek and we officially entered Cairo on foot. We walked down El Tahrir street then took a left towards Gezira street. The view of the Cairo Tower had been visible since we were in El Nile Street.

I told Younes, "We want to pass by the tower and take a photo there."

It was an important landmark, and for me it was a symbol that we had really reached Cairo. Younes talked with the event management company and we spontaneously took a left onto Al Borg street, which is a narrow road with a huge, very old tree in the middle. We didn't have any approval to walk in this street but by the time the police realized this, it was too late and we were already taking a photo in front of the tower. They allowed us to stay there for only five minutes so we couldn't take photos with the rest of the teams. It was only the five of us in the picture, jumping. Then we left quickly and took a right onto El Gabalaya street, where our final destination was.

I looked at Younes and told him that he can wake up now. He understood immediately what I was referring to. One of Avicii's songs that we must have heard over fifty times was "Wake Me Up." In the main stanza of the song Avicii asks to be waked up when all is over, then he will be wiser and older. He has been trying to find himself though he didn't know he was lost.

In our life journey, we don't know the end, but we have an idea of what to do in the moment. In this journey, each one of us got closer to finding him or herself—even if it wasn't what we were searching for. And yes we also got older; we lived the equivalent of one year in twenty-four days. Living this journey had made us more mature and stronger, both physically and mentally. I know that mental resilience has a direct effect on physical health and vice versa but there is also another factor that has an effect on our mental health: mindfulness and compassion.

We reached the El Gezira youth center. We were welcomed by the youth there, as well as reporters, and most importantly for me, my parents were there waiting for me. I went over to them and we hugged, then I introduced them to the team. My mum was so proud of me and my dad discovered for the first time that I had walked the entire distance at the ceremony. Whenever my father had called me, I had waited until I was in the car or back from the walk to call him back. This was so that when I told him that I was in the car or in my room, it wouldn't be a lie. Otherwise if I had taken his calls while walking and trying to catch my breath, especially in the first few days when my heart rate was high, he would have been very worried about me all the time. A reporter came to take a photo of me with my parents, and another one took my mum's number to call her for an interview.

There was a ceremony organized for us. We were honored by the Ministry of Youth and given medals and certificates. In the certificates, the distance each one of us walked was mentioned, but Ahmed preferred not to disclose that information. In the ceremony I found my younger sister entering the hall with her two sons. The eldest was three years old and he came running over to me. This was the best reward I had that day.

After the ceremony we went for lunch at the youth center. Younes came to sit beside me and he apologized for the calculation mistake but I told him that it was for the best. If we had had a rest day, we would not have reached the ceremony on time.

After lunch, I asked Osama for a word. I told him about Hamdy's work proposal and I wanted his opinion. I know that Osama talked with everyone and I thought he might know something or have some insight. Moreover, he is self-employed, he started from scratch, and dealt with all kinds of people so I wanted his advice. Osama looked worried and told me that he would get back to me. At night, on our way to dinner, he told me that he had asked around and he understood what was happening. He had called Sally, the girl that had been hired in the first week of the challenge and disappeared. She hadn't wanted to tell him in the beginning what had happened, but after he told her that I had a job offer, she told him that the reason she had left so suddenly is because she was harassed.

For dinner, we went to Sequoia, a Middle Eastern restaurant overlooking the Nile with a warm and friendly atmosphere. We had a long table reserved for us. Hamdy sat beside me and Ramzy in front of him, between Osama and Younes, Mohsen beside me from the other side.I felt that their presence divided the team. I knew that Hamdy was waiting for me to give him my decision, but after the news Osama had told me I decided that I would not even tell him that I was not interested except if he asked.

Each of us ordered, and while waiting for the food I remembered my dream of the previous night. "Younes," I called to him over Hamdy and Ramzy, "last night I had a bad dream. I dreamt that we were going to our start point but we got lost and we went 30 km further."

He laughed and we all laughed.

After dinner, Hamdy left so did some of the support team. I asked them if they want to move to a smaller table closer to the Nile and we have some tea. Ramzy came to sit by my side and Younes and Osama were just in front of us. Ramzy asked me about my plans after the challenge. I knew that he wanted to know if I was interested in the offer. I told him that I didn't know yet and I didn't want to think about it then. He suddenly wanted us to leave. Younes interrupted, looking at me. "Don't you want to have tea." We had some and Ramzy asked for the bill as soon as we were done and we left.

At the hotel we got into the elevator. Each one of us left at our respective floors and we said our goodbyes. It was like trains at a station, each time one of us left for our destination. Younes and I were the last two. When my turn to leave came, we didn't say goodbye—but simply, till we meet again.

On February the 8th, Helmy Elsaeed and Jomana Ismail set a record of crossing from Aswan to Cairo on foot, covering 900 km in 24 days. They wouldn't have been able to do that without their supporting team. The walk was sponsored by the United Nations Population Fund (UNFP).

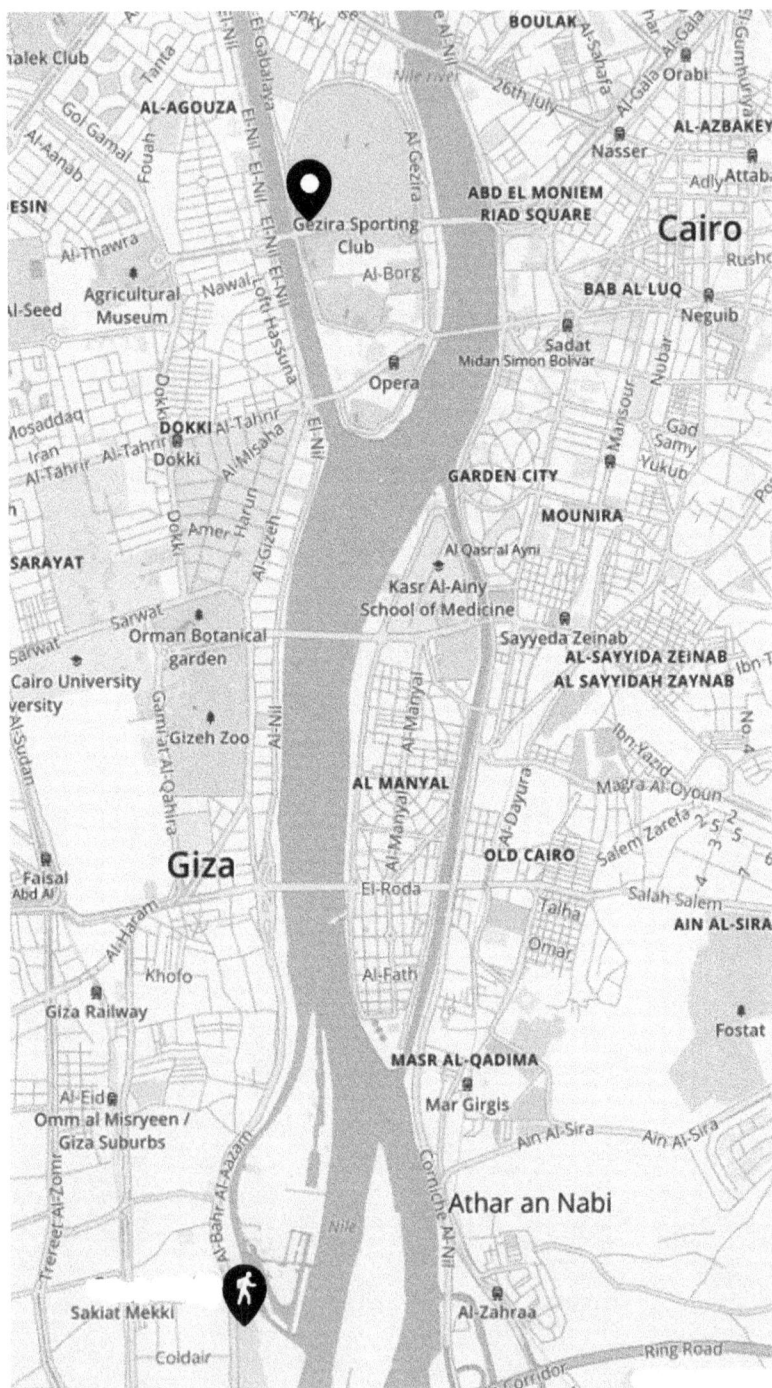

Jomana Ismail was raised in Cairo, Egypt in a middle class family. Her parents are always supportive. She is the middle child between two sisters and that gave her the privilege to be the younger sister and the older sister; she has the backbone and the kind heartedness.

Jomana has an MBA from Leipzig University. She had colleagues from 23 countries from most of the continents. This exposure gave her the privilege to review her convictions and values and adopt ones of her own. Sports have always been part of Jomana's life. She performed artistic gymnastics when she was a young girl. Currently, she does standup paddle and won the national championship, she hikes, and practices Yoga.

www.ingramcontent.com/pod-product-compliance
Lightning Source LLC
Chambersburg PA
CBHW030714110426
42739CB00029B/154